ENGAGING VIRTUAL ENVIRONMENTS

ENGAGING VIRTUAL ENVIRONMENTS

Creative Ideas and Online Tools to Promote Student

Interaction, Participation, and Active Learning

Joanne Ricevuto and Laura McLaughlin

Foreword by Lillian Nave

STERLING, VIRGINIA

Published by Stylus Publishing, LLC.
22883 Quicksilver Drive
Sterling, Virginia 20166-2019

Library of Congress Cataloging-in-Publication-Data

Names: Ricevuto, Joanne, author. | McLaughlin, Laura, author.
Title: Engaging virtual environments : creative ideas and online tools to promote student interaction, participation, and active learning / Joanne Ricevuto and Laura McLaughlin ; Foreword by Lillian Nave.
Description: First edition. | Sterling, Virginia : Stylus Publishing, LLC, [2022] | Includes bibliographical references and index. | Summary: "This book will help you connect with students, whether you're teaching synchronously or asynchronously, regardless of the devices students may be using; develop community; and introduce you to gamification to add enjoyment and variety to your students' experience of your class"-- Provided by publisher.
Identifiers: LCCN 2022019550 (print) | LCCN 2022019551 (ebook) | ISBN 9781642673883 (cloth) | ISBN 9781642673890 (paperback) | ISBN 9781642673906 (pdf) | ISBN 9781642673913 (epub)
Subjects: LCSH: Virtual reality in education. | Effective teaching. | Active learning. | Gamification. | Motivation in education.
Classification: LCC LB1044.87 .R52 2022 (print) | LCC LB1044.87 (ebook) | DDC 371.33468--dc23
LC record available at https://lccn.loc.gov/2022019550
LC ebook record available at https://lccn.loc.gov/2022019551

13-digit ISBN: 978-1-64267-388-3 (cloth)
13-digit ISBN: 978-1-64267-389-0 (paperback)
13-digit ISBN: 978-1-64267-390-6 (library networkable e-edition)
13-digit ISBN: 978-1-64267-391-3 (consumer e-edition)

Printed in the United States of America

All first editions printed on acid-free paper
that meets the American National Standards Institute
Z39-48 Standard.

Bulk Purchases

Quantity discounts are available for use in workshops and for staff development.

Call 1-800-232-0223

First Edition, 2022

CONTENTS

FOREWORD

Recently an enormous shift has taken place in institutions of higher education in which the typical in-person classroom has been abruptly moved online because of a worldwide pandemic. Professors and instructors who have taught for 20 years or just 2 months had to radically change their delivery method and rethink how they could reach their students in this new educational environment. However, this "emergency remote" instruction does not compare to a true understanding of the capacity, flexibility, and transformational experience that an online or virtual classroom can accomplish. In the rush to move online, too often instructors translate their in-person teaching to a semimodified classroom-like experience that can often leave students feeling disconnected, disengaged, and wanting more because the design of the course was never for the online environment. *Engaging Virtual Environments: Practical Tips and Strategies for Connecting and Collaborating in a Virtual Environment* by Joanne Ricevuto and Laura McLaughlin offers a solution to this problem that is innovative, well-designed, and easily adapted by anyone teaching in the online environment today.

Ricevuto and McLaughlin provide the rationale behind what it means to be a virtual instructor in every facet the role entails. They describe the many hats that a virtual instructor must wear in order to design, build, facilitate, and evaluate a collaborative, engaging virtual learning experience. Each chapter is divided into two sections. The first part of each chapter explores the related roles or facets of a virtual instructor, and the second section provides tips, tools, and templates to help the instructor in each one of these roles.

First, the roles of the virtual instructor range from being the decision maker and facilitator, to course designer and student engager, and finally the lifelong learner and knowledge sharer. Traditionally, we think of the major role of the instructor to be the "knowledge sharer," or "one who professes," but Ricevuto and McLaughlin turn that concept on its ear to show how many other roles the virtual instructor must fulfill even before sharing the knowledge that they have so long gathered. The authors have taken no shortcuts here and have laid out myriad ways to conceptualize what must happen as the virtual instructor conceptualizes the course, plans the outcomes, and determines how to facilitate meaningful interactions between students and the instructor, students and the material, and among students. Several chapters focus on the responsibility the instructor has of engaging students as project planner, course designer, and assessor while other chapters tackle the important characteristics a successful virtual instructor must have that include being a lifelong learner, a content expert, and a knowledge sharer. But where many other online learning books often fail is where Ricevuto and McLaughlin shine—in the facilitation aspects of being a virtual instructor as a community builder and supporter, team builder, student engager, collaborator, and importantly, a diversity, equity and inclusion (DEI) guide. These roles have been overlooked in both in-person and online guides in the past, and the authors here do the important work of teasing out all of the ways in which the virtual instructor must approach the design, assessments, interactions, and most importantly, the facilitation of the course.

Second, after the particular roles in each chapter are delineated, the authors offer tip after tip, and tool after tool to make sure that during the course itself, the materials are accessible, the students are included, and everyone is engaged in the learning process. Ricevuto and McLaughlin have a thorough understanding of the universal design for learning (UDL) guidelines and emphasize their use throughout the book in order to create an inclusive, equitable, warm, and inviting educational experience for all. Here is where the good intentions of a well-built course are put to the test—in the execution of these roles—and this book provides everything one would need. Each chapter offers multiple options and a clear plan of action so that the virtual instructor is prepared and equipped to engage every student from the first session to the final goodbye.

Engaging Virtual Environments: Practical Tips and Strategies for Connecting and Collaborating in a Virtual Environment systematically delineates the many facets of the role of the instructor in the online environment today. Before sharing one's expertise, the virtual instructor must design the course from start to finish, determine learning outcomes, choose assessments to match those learning outcomes, select appropriate technology, make sure that the course is accessible and inclusive, and facilitate the learning and provide feedback throughout the course. It is a very tall order and the authors have beautifully constructed a step-by-step process to guide the new virtual instructor through this complicated process. Indeed, this book is a veritable decision tree for the new or "not-so-new" virtual instructor that includes helpful definitions, appropriate questions to ask oneself along the way, and many tips, tools, and templates to make teaching online fun and satisfying for the instructor, and interesting and engaging for the student. It is an essential tool to have in the virtual instructor's toolbox for today's challenging online teaching and learning environment.

—Lillian Nave
Senior Lecturer and Universal Design for
Learning Coordinator at Appalachian State University
and Host of Think UDL Podcast

INTRODUCTION

Creating Engaging, Inspiring, Flexible
Virtual Environments

The beautiful thing about learning is that no one can take it away from you.

—BB King

The U.S. Department of Education (2017) report, *Reimagining the Role of Technology in Higher Education*, stated: "unless we become nimbler in our approach and more scalable in our solutions, we will miss out on an opportunity to embrace and serve the majority of students who will need higher education and postsecondary learning" (p. 8). The message in this report calls us to find ways to serve our students and provide an engaging, flexible environment. Emerging technology can help us do just that but getting started may seem challenging. As we will reiterate many times throughout this book, we want to provide information you can use right away to enhance what you are already doing in your virtual classrooms. As faculty members ourselves, we know that teaching in a virtual environment can sometimes feel overwhelming. However, if we identify the best tools, collaborate with colleagues, and embrace a growth mindset, we believe we can create an online environment that is engaging, flexible, and inspiring for our students. Throughout the chapters, we will share quotes we gathered in our research from faculty we surveyed about their experiences teaching in a virtual environment. We share these perspectives because we know that faculty voices are needed as we move forward with virtual instruction and continue to improve our practice while creating environments that are engaging, flexible, and meeting the needs of our diverse learners (Figure I.1).

Whether you have been teaching online for a decade or are new at online teaching or haven't even started yet, we all, most likely, have the same goal of creating environments where our students are learning and where we can teach to the best of our abilities. Although this all sounds so simple, our own experiences, our own research, and research we have gathered from others tells us it is not that simple. According to the International Council for Open and Distance Education (2018), virtual learning may be perceived worldwide as

1

Figure I.1. Engaging, inspiring, flexible online environments.

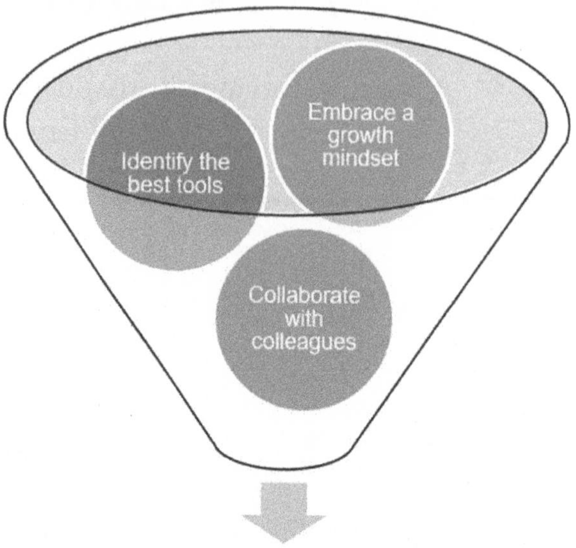

Note. Creating engaging, inspiring, and flexible virtual environments consists of identifying the best tool, collaborating with colleagues, and having a growth mindset—not in any specific order.

being less effective than face-to-face learning, professional development and support within the organization may be lacking, and concerns with either a lack of quality standards used or the inconsistent use of quality standards when designing virtual instruction may be present. There are many barriers to creating this engaging, inspiring, flexible environment. Many times, faculty may feel isolated and lack the time or ability to collaborate with colleagues. There may be competitiveness or fear of failure due to the culture that is present within a particular institution. In academia, faculty may be expected to research, advise, publish, teach, and be seen as leaders in both their communities and their institutions. The expectations and pressures placed on faculty may cause them to miss opportunities to invest in the time it takes to create these environments.

The Boston Consulting Group (BCG, 2018) highlighted successes from six higher education institutions when it came to online teaching and learning. They reported "faculty may worry (perhaps rightfully so) about course quality, poor outcomes, the time commitment involved, and their own inexperience with the modality" (p. 34). The findings from this study also found that when institutions took a strategic approach to building a high-quality digital environment, there were three key impacts: (a) equivalent or improved student learning outcomes; (b) increased access, especially to disadvantaged students; and (c) increased revenues (BCG, 2018). Because of these promising findings, we need to continue to work hard at creating engaging, flexible, and inspiring virtual environments where our students, our institutions, and we can continue to grow. Hopefully, institutions will continue to find ways to invest in a strategic approach that includes supporting faculty and students in these important efforts. Interestingly, the Online Learning Consortium (OLC, 2016) reported that even when institutions strategically plan digital learning growth, faculty are sometimes hesitant to embrace these efforts.

According to our research, over 60% of our respondents stated that 2020 was the first time they were teaching virtually, and this was due to the global pandemic. As we move forward, we believe that virtual teaching and learning will not be going away and when given resources and the support needed to implement effective online teaching, we will be able to increase access and accommodations and offer flexible, engaging ways for students to learn. Our goal is to relieve some of this worry and hesitancy by providing support and practical tips to make this process easier and less time consuming.

Our Approach to This Book

Learning, as we commonly know it, is constantly changing. When students are in a classroom setting, interaction among students is inevitable; however, in a virtual setting, this is not the case. But all is not lost in a virtual setting, because although you are not meeting in person, that does not mean that you cannot facilitate interaction and engagement among students. The setting has changed, but not the purpose.

We have many years of experience in the classroom due to our backgrounds in teacher education and teaching in higher education for over 20 years. We also have extensive experience in faculty development and presenting workshops to improve the teaching and learning on our respective campuses. This book is written *by* teachers *for* teachers! We are going to help you create real connections to your students in your virtual classroom through the three T's: tips, tools, and templates. *Although we are coming from a teacher education background, the ideas we share can be modified and used for any content area.* Our work with faculty includes faculty across disciplines and content areas.

Primary Audience

Our primary audience for this book is any educator who is teaching virtually. Although our current positions are within higher education, the three T's will be applicable to any educational setting, as well as for trainers in any field who need to find ways to engage their audiences. Our biggest push is to offer ideas that will help you better engage your audiences with activities and assessments that are relevant and enjoyable. Students will be more apt to turn their cameras on and participate if you are doing an activity that is easy to engage in and perform on any type of electronic device.

With virtual learning here to stay, we have the unique opportunity to rethink and reinvent teaching in higher education. In fact, with the right approach, technology, and mindset, we can overcome some of the challenges that have plagued teaching in higher education for many years. So, our book will provide you with many ways to enhance your classes, regardless of being a first-time online teacher, one that was a survivor of the pandemic teacher, or one that just wants to find new ways to engage their learners.

Structure of Our Book

We are going to introduce tips, tools, and templates that we use and/or have created that will be useful in a virtual setting, but also can be modified for a face-to-face setting. We know that faculty play many roles and although we cannot cover them all, we focused on roles we felt were most important in a virtual environment. Each chapter will begin with a discussion regarding a specific role or roles faculty fill in virtual learning environments and what tools we have found to be most helpful in accomplishing the specific roles. We will share information we gathered from our own experience and from the research we have gathered.

Roles of Faculty Members in Virtual Teaching and Learning

The roles discussed within each chapter are as follows:

- chapter 1: decision maker and facilitator
- chapter 2: community builder and supporter
- chapter 3: team builder, learner, and collaborator
- chapter 4: course designer and student engager
- chapter 5: content expert and diversity, equity, and inclusion guide
- chapter 6: project planner and assessor
- chapter 7: lifelong learner and knowledge sharer

Each of our chapters has two parts. In the second part of our chapter, we provide specific tips, tools, and/or templates to guide you as you fulfill your many roles as a virtual instructor. The ideas are meant to be quick and easy to implement and practical. You don't have to use every idea—just use the ones that resonate with you. Almost all the ideas we share are free to use, most do not require you to download anything, and they are only encouraged to be used if they will help you create more engaging virtual environments.

Tips, Tools, and Templates

The second part of each chapter will consist of practical examples you can use right away if you choose. We call this section Tips, Tools, and Templates and hope to provide you with ideas you can use right away in your virtual environments.

Additionally, we will encourage you to utilize your learning management system (LMS) and to see which of our ideas can be automatically and easily embedded within your LMS and course pages. These tools are generally available as "apps" within your LMS platform. Each LMS is different, but you could find out how to easily embed these tools so that you don't have to download from an outside source. For instance, in Canvas, you would access your course on your dashboard, click on settings, and then click on the "apps" tab. Once you are in the "apps" tab, you are able to search the tools that are available to embed within the system. However, you would need to find out for your specific LMS platform how to embed apps within your system.

If appropriate, we include step-by-step instructions to using a specific tool, along with screenshots, as well as providing a QR code to a template. From our work with faculty development, we have found that sometimes providing specific step-by-step directions or a template may help faculty to take the next step in trying something out. If you are an iPhone or Android user, you can simply click onto your camera and hover over the QR code. It will automatically link you to the website and/or template.

Guide to Tools Section

We included a Guide to Tools section that provides a table listing 50 tools we discuss within this book along with QR codes for each, links, a short description of the tool, and chapters/pages where the tools are mentioned. We know there are so many more tools out there and available, but we picked 50 that we use most frequently and found most helpful when engaging our virtual learners. We know tools change and as continual learners and collaborators, we wanted to also provide an ongoing resource, the supplemental guide.

Supplemental Guide

We provide access to a supplemental guide where we have added additional resources that we could not fit within this book. The supplemental guide is a work in progress, and we will continue to add resources even after this book is published. The guide is organized by the book chapters and content areas. We welcome our readers to share ideas with us that we can include within our supplemental guide. You can access the Google folder by going to the Virtual Instruction Support for Faculty Google folder, and it can be accessed by scanning the QR code we provide in Figure I.2 or going to https://tinyurl.com/VISF-folder to collaborate and share ideas with each other. You are free to use, copy, modify, and share any resources within these folders. Any of the templates we share within the book will also be shared within this supplemental guide and found within the respective chapter folder. We plan to continue to update this supplemental guide because we know tools change and directions change, but our desire to engage virtual learners won't change.

Each of the chapters will include a table (Table I.1) that will address the terms *social presence, teaching presence,* and *cognitive presence* and provide examples of how these presences may be integrated within a virtual environment. These three presences make up the community of inquiry framework and when all three presences are available within an online course, a collaborative and constructive learning experience occurs (Garrison et al., 2000). Garrison (2007) stated, "higher education has consistently viewed community as essential to support collaborative learning and discourse associated with higher levels of learning" (p. 61). We consider this community of inquiry framework essential in creating engaging virtual environments. We will highlight which presences will be covered in each chapter, and you will

Figure I.2. Online teaching resources Google folder.

see many of the items overlap each other. We will suggest tools and strategies we use to create engaging virtual environments that consist of a combination of social, teaching, and cognitive presence. However, we want to stress that although we will suggest specific tools that we use, tools are constantly changing. We use new tools all the time. We have some tools we continually use because they work well for us and help us meet our learning goals. We have tools we may have tried once and realized it wasn't for us or we preferred another tool. We learn about the tools we use from a variety of sources including other faculty, conferences we attend, research we have done, classes we have taken, our students, and sometimes our own children. We are constantly learning and developing as virtual instructors and we encourage you to do the same. Our focus is not on the tool, but it is on creating engaging virtual environments where our students thrive and learn.

TABLE I.1

Examples of the Community of Inquiry Framework in Virtual Instruction: Social, Teaching, and Cognitive Presence

Social Presence	Teaching Presence	Cognitive Presence
Getting to know other students	Getting to know the teacher	Making sense of the content
Expressing emotions and opinions	One-on-one meetings/conversations with the teacher	Discussing the content for further understanding
Creating opportunities for collaboration	Asking the teacher questions	Digging deeper and taking part in project-based learning, service learning, research
Sharing a story	Engaging with teacher-directed assignments	Having students respond to other students
Building classroom community; supporting each other	Introducing a topic or project	Sharing knowledge and work with each other
Check-ins	Planning and preparing online course for student engagement	Providing peer feedback
Creating a sense of belonging	Creating an environment that is authentic and supportive	Using multimodal modes of instruction—videos, readings, resources

Additionally, we are highly complementary of the OLC and their work to develop scorecards for online teaching and learning, and we have used their scorecards to guide us as we plan for virtual instruction. The OLC (2016) Quality Course Teaching and Instructional Practice scorecard is one that we encourage you to download and refer to as well. OLC provides instructors with the necessary criteria and benchmarking tools to ensure online learning excellence. This scorecard will focus on four different areas and can be used for an in-depth assessment of instructional practices. The scorecard is broken down into the following areas: course fundamentals, learning foundations, faculty engagement, and student engagement. As we have worked through these self-assessment tools and continue to become better virtual instructors ourselves, we could not help but notice the diverse roles that faculty members need to fill while planning and teaching in a virtual environment. For this reason, we organized our chapters around the roles of the faculty member. There are so many roles that we had to decide which ones to focus on in the context of virtual learning.

Scorecards are accessible through this link or QR code (Figure I.3):

https://onlinelearningconsortium.org/consult/olc-quality-course-teaching-instructional-practice/

The book consists of the Guide to Tools and seven chapters. The Guide to Tools can be used as a resource while reading through this book and can help you access the tools we discuss easily and quickly. We provide the following description of each chapter, and the chapters can be read in any order.

Figure I.3. Scan this QR code to access OLC quality scorecard on quality course teaching and instructional practice.

Chapter One: Virtual Instructor as Decision Maker and Facilitator

In this chapter, we will discuss strategies we use to decide on how to best engage our students with the use of tools either within our LMS or outside of our LMS. We will focus on the purpose of a tool and how it will enhance the learning experience. It will also include a QR code that will link to a template to utilize on deciding whether a new tool is appropriate for what you want to accomplish. Tools are a great way to enhance your virtual learning space; however, instructors have to decide when would be the best time to use a particular tool, and when to introduce the students, for we don't want to overwhelm them either. We also know that a large part of this decision process is embedded in mindsets, and we discuss the need for mindsets such as flexibility, innovation, and risk-taking for both ourselves and our students. As a virtual instructor, the role of the faculty is one of a facilitator/coach who supports students to become self-directed and confident learners and we provide tips on ways to do this within the virtual environment while building cognitive presence leading to deeper learning.

Chapter Two: Virtual Instructor as Community Builder and Supporter

We will focus on providing tips, tools, and templates on how to create a space that is positive for social emotional learning, which will include check-ins with our students. The chapter will begin with how to create a landing page, so that students feel welcome as soon as they log into Zoom or whatever platform you use, along with hearing background music. Students want a strong connection with their professors. It often fuels their excitement to learn when they have a connection to their professor through formal and informal interactions and communication. So, we will provide tools to use like Padlet, Jamboard, Canva, and so on to establish this type of connection, and to enhance your virtual classroom. Additionally, humor is touched on and how you can add it to your virtual environment.

Chapter Three: Virtual Instructor as Team Member, Learner, and Collaborator

In this chapter, we discuss the role of the virtual instructor as a team builder, learner, and collaborator—someone who connects with colleagues and peers to find ways to learn together and grow. The virtual instructor in the role of a team builder, learner, and collaborator not only connects with others but finds ways to help learners connect with each other in teams where they learn and collaborate. These teams can be formed through group projects that are developed and assigned to learners or informally where learners have opportunities within their virtual environment to interact and work with others. Within these team environments, virtual instructors have opportunities to build teaching presence as well as social and cognitive presence.

Chapter Four: Virtual Instructor as Course Designer and Student Engager

Within this chapter, we will focus on how to provide an engaging virtual space during synchronous sessions. For students to be engaged during synchronous virtual learning, information needs to be at both the instructor's and students' fingertips. In this chapter, there will be many tools that will be mentioned to create an engaging space, as well as how we can use gamification and using platforms like Kahoot! to keep our students engaged. These tools will be easy to use, manipulate, and access, which will make teaching synchronously enjoyable to both the students and instructors.

Chapter Five: Virtual Instructor as Content Expert and Diversity, Equity, and Inclusion Guide

Within this chapter, we will focus on building content knowledge specifically with asynchronous instruction. We believe asynchronous instruction allows learners to engage with the content in the most effective and flexible ways and that asynchronous content presentation helps to increase cognition, remove educational barriers, and build social, teaching, and cognitive presence within a virtual environment. In addition, virtual instructors can increase accessibility through universal design and awareness of the need for diversity, equity, and inclusion within course design, course materials, and course instruction. This chapter will support how asynchronous sessions allow flexibility and may provide greater access and diversity to our students. Platforms that will be mentioned include VoiceThread, Nearpod, Pear Deck, and so forth.

Chapter Six: Virtual Instructor as Project Planner and Assessor

This chapter will focus on how virtual instructors can create environments that engage learners and assess their learning in creative and alternative ways. Assessment should drive our decisions, so students should be given an opportunity to show what they know through assessments that work best in a virtual environment. Assessing learners solely through tests and quizzes does not work best in a virtual environment. Assessments should include things like choice, tying assessment to the course purpose, as well as allowing for creativity and innovation.

Chapter Seven: Virtual Instructor as Lifelong Learner and Knowledge Sharer

This chapter focuses on how instructors can continue to grow and to utilize information that they have learned in this book to become a more refined virtual instructor. The tool choices will only continue to grow as will resources available to virtual instructors to help them engage their learners. We know that learning in a virtual environment removes barriers such as being tied to a specific time to learn, place to learn, and the people we learn with. As virtual instructors, we have access to 24/7 learning with people we would never have imagined learning with. We encourage you to take the opportunity to network with other virtual instructors and share ideas with each other. We provide suggestions on how to do this within this chapter.

Reflection Questions

At the end of each chapter, we provide reflection questions that can be used to discuss each chapter either individually or within a faculty learning community. We hope you will use these questions to drive conversation and work together to support each other in virtual teaching and learning and support each other in fulfilling the many roles you play as a virtual instructor.

Between the two of us, we use different strategies ourselves and acknowledge that not everything will work in every environment. One of us cannot imagine teaching a course without using VoiceThread, the other does not use VoiceThread. We both use different LMSs and different cloud-based video conferencing platforms. One of us works within an LMS where many of the tools are embedded, while the other one has little to no tools embedded within the LMS. One of us prefers synchronous instruction, while the other prefers asynchronous with some synchronous instruction. However, both of us are passionate about virtual learning, have years of experience doing it ourselves, and are dedicated to supporting faculty in their many roles as virtual instructors. We recognize the diversity we all bring into our virtual teaching and learning and we can all learn from each other. In what follows we provide two examples of the practical ideas that will be within each chapter.

The best way to improve your practice is *practice*! So, how do you practice online teaching (for a synchronous class)? Depending on your virtual platform, there are ways to practice an online session without an audience.

Figure I.4. Zoom personal room.

Meetings

Upcoming   Previous   Personal Room   Meeting Templates

📅 Start Time   to   End Time

Figure I.5. Start button to open your personal Zoom room.

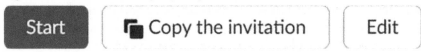

Find out if your platform provides a personal room where you can practice using the tools that you want to try before an actual session.

If you are using Zoom as your platform, there is a place under My Meetings that is called Personal Room (Figure I.4).

Hover your mouse over the Personal Room and click on it. Once you click on it, you will see information about your personal ID, but at the bottom of the screen on the left, you will see a blue Start button. Click on the Start button, and your own personal Zoom will begin (Figure I.5).

Once you are in your own personal Zoom, you can practice all the things you want to do in your next online synchronous class. Try out your virtual backgrounds, filters, settings, and so on. There are a few items you can't do when it's only you in the session, including immersive view, polls, and break-out rooms. If you wish to practice using these features, ask some friends to join in. We often would ask our children and their friends to join in and then we would try out a bunch of new features with them. Then they would just stay on and talk to each other, so it was a win-win situation.

Additionally, when we would teach each synchronous session, we would have a green screen behind us. You can find them very cheap on Amazon. so that we were able to change our virtual background throughout the class, as well as have a second monitor to use for what the students would see on their screens if we were screen sharing. Then on our laptop screen would be the Zoom controls along with all of the windows opened that we planned on using that class period. When we were ready to show one of the windows, we would drag it over to the monitor screen. This made for an easy transition with what was being shown on the screen.

We also would have our cell phones next to the monitor and laptop and logged into the Zoom session with the camera and sound off. We used the cell phone so we could see exactly what the students were seeing as well as hearing, so we didn't have to say, "Does everybody see this?" and "Does everybody hear this?"

The Syllabus in the Virtual Environment

The syllabus, as we know it, changes in a virtual environment. Gone are the days of printing out 30 copies of a 20-page syllabus and going through this document with students on the 1st day of class. We embed our syllabus within our LMS where our students can access it and where we include important elements of our virtual classroom. We provide a tentative course outline where learners can see all that we plan to do within our course, but also with the understanding that things can change. What does not change within our course is the course learning outcomes and goals of our course. We have learned that information about what is due and when it is due should be in multiple places within the virtual learning environment and learners should receive announcement reminders and support in being successful in the virtual environment. We have found that many times our learners are not used to being as self-directed in a virtual environment, so there is a need for scaffolding and flexibility, which we will discuss throughout this book.

To create a more engaging syllabus, you can use a screen-sharing tool such as Loom or Screencastify to share your screen and talk through the syllabus while it is on the screen and then share the video with your students. Your students can then comment on the video and ask for clarification so that this is an interactive process. You can also create your syllabus using VoiceThread and upload your syllabus into VoiceThread and then voice or video record yourself going through the syllabus, capturing key information, and then asking students to also interact with the syllabus. Regardless of the tool you use to do this, the idea is to transform the way you engage your students in a virtual environment. We hope this book provides you with many ways to do this as you manage the multiple roles of the virtual instructor.

The collaborative nature of this effort in writing this book draws on best practices identified through our research and experiences. As you work through this book, we hope you will find the information, which is grounded in research and our own experience, practical and easy to use, and hopefully it will enhance your virtual teaching practice. With the successful adoption of the tips, tools, and templates suggested in this book, our hope is that you will be able to improve student engagement, ensure student accessibility, and improve student learning and assessment and have fun while doing all these things.

Wrapping It Up

Although our job titles do not include instructional design experts, we do have a lot of experience in teaching and we will walk you through each of these chapters with many tips, tools, and templates that will help you become an exemplary virtual instructor. We know there are high expectations for virtual instructors with a multitude of roles to fill—ones we may have not expected to have to fill. We acknowledge this and hope that you gain practical ideas you can use right away to help you engage your learners. We want to provide you with a better understanding of the relevant technologies that are available to instructors to enhance virtual environments. We hope to provide you with the confidence to try something new and to step out of your comfort zone. Rome wasn't built overnight, and things take time. Be aware that you will not become proficient immediately in all the ideas that are provided to you. You need to accept that with any new idea that you try out, it might fail, but that is okay. Students are more likely to accept a failed new idea if you are up front and tell them you want to try something new with them.

One word to remember to improve your skill as a virtual instructor is practice! You will not become an expert virtual instructor overnight; it will take lots of practice and patience to try these new ideas out. But taking the first step and being brave enough to try something new is a step in the right direction.

Learning can and should be fun . . . even in higher education! Use the innovative ideas in this book and integrate them into your online teaching practice, because this will offer you a pathway to transform your teaching.

VIRTUAL INSTRUCTOR AS DECISION MAKER AND FACILITATOR

The most difficult thing is the decision to act, the rest is merely tenacity.

—Amelia Earhart

In this chapter, we will discuss the role of the virtual instructor as a decision maker and facilitator. The virtual instructor uses strategies to decide on how to best engage students with the use of tools either within their LMS or outside the LMS. We provide templates to help with these decisions and deciding on the tool to use. In addition, the virtual instructor serves as a facilitator/coach who supports students to become self-directed and confident learners and we provide tips on ways to do this within the virtual environment while building cognitive presence leading to deeper learning.

Part 1: The Virtual Instructor as Decision Maker and Facilitator

Before we dive in, let us define what we mean by a *decision maker or facilitator* to ensure we are providing clarity in thinking about these roles as they appear in similar contexts. In the context of virtual teaching and learning, the role of decision maker includes decisions about what content is being taught and how that content is being taught. We cannot possibly cover all decisions that faculty make regarding course design and pedagogical strategies within this book; however, we do want to discuss the role of virtual instructors as decision makers when it specifically relates to virtual engagement of learners in their courses. Our goal here is to provide a structure that you can use when deciding on tools or strategies to engage our virtual learners. We also want to clarify that the roles we discuss within this book are not linear, meaning they happen in a certain sequence. There are many times when you can use information provided within this chapter while filling other roles we discuss throughout this book. For example, we provide a template at the end of this chapter we use when making decisions about what tools to use (Table 1.3), and this template can be used and will be referred to in other chapters within this book. We provide a QR code in Figure 1.2 where you can access and use this template as you evaluate tools you plan to use, and this template is also provided within our supplemental guide noted in the Introduction of the book. The roles we cover within this book overlap and so the material we write about in one chapter may also be relevant in another chapter—use what works for you.

When we refer to the role of a virtual instructor as a *facilitator*, we define this as the virtual instructor planning, guiding, supporting, and coaching their learners. This is a role that begins before a course starts and remains even after a course ends. A central theme of our book is that virtual instruction is a way to remove barriers of time, space, and access. In the past, instruction occurred at a certain time, in a certain place, but now learning can and does occur continuously throughout a course, even extending after a course ends. For example, we discuss the use of shared folders, discussion pages, and resources that are outside of your institution's LMS where learners can continue to access the information and contribute to the learning even after the course ends.

Within this chapter, in addition, we discuss the mindsets that support virtual instructors, but we recognize that these mindsets apply to all of the roles we discuss within this book, not just for the roles in this chapter. The ideas and tools we describe throughout this book can be modified to work within your discipline and content area. We share how we specifically do this with the hope that this will spark creativity and innovation as you figure out how this can work within your own virtual setting.

Decision-Making: Aligning Tools to Course Purpose and Faculty Role

You have many decisions to make even before meeting your students and setting up your course in a virtual environment. Although we will suggest many ideas and specific tools we have used as virtual instructors, we suggest that the most important thing to do is to align your choices of tools to the purpose and desired outcomes of your course. Some decisions are made for you, such as the learning management systems and video conferencing tools available to you through our institutions, and then it seems as though the rest is up to you. This can become overwhelming when there is so much to choose from and when we are unsure where to start to make these decisions.

The tools and suggestions provided here should make this process easier and having a mindset that embraces flexibility and adaptability is a key to successful decision-making and facilitation of virtual teaching and learning.

As learners become more self-directed and responsible for their learning in a virtual environment, not only does the learner's role change, but the role of the instructor changes as well (Berge, 2008). With learners having continuous access to information and knowledge through online sources and each other, the instructor moves from expert and sole provider of knowledge sharing to one of a facilitator and coach (Berge, 2008). Referring to this shift in roles within a virtual environment, Cunningham (2010) noted, "No longer is the 'teaching event' in the hands of the instructor alone. The student shares half if not more of that responsibility" (p. 92). This role change affects the decisions related to the tools used in a virtual environment. As facilitators of a virtual environment, you will want to see learners as self-directed, critical thinkers who want (and deserve) a say in how they engage in their own learning and are given a multitude of choices in their learning (Henrikson, 2020).

Decisions on Learning Management Systems and Video Conferencing Tools

As professors, both of us use a learning management system (LMS), but we use different ones at our institutions. These are increasingly powerful tools, and we recommend learning to use them well. It is likely you have access to an LMS to organize your course materials and to communicate with the learners in the course, and your LMS is likely to be the foundational tool for your course. In addition, most of us now have access to a video conferencing (VC) tool such as Zoom, Teams, Meet, or WebEx, and usually more than one.

The capabilities of these tools vary greatly, and we will not spend much time on the use of an individual LMS or VC tool, but we believe it is important to use the tools you have access to through your institutions. For purposes of discussion, we will assume that every LMS includes a basic capability to present the syllabus elements, make announcements, facilitate discussion, and support grade collection. We will assume a VC tool includes the capabilities to hold virtual group discussions and to present information in both a desktop or mobile browser and via an audio-only connection. A VC tool with breakout rooms is highly useful, as we will discuss, but that capability is not always possible and there are ways around that limitation if your VC tool lacks this capability.

We strongly believe that to fully engage your virtual learners in a virtual environment, you need to explore modalities outside of the LMS and

VC tools. Some institutions integrate outside tools within their LMS, and some do not. Whatever your situation, we provide ideas for you to try that are simple, free, and fun with the goal of creating engaging virtual environments both inside and outside of your defined LMS or VC environment.

And in case you do not have access to an LMS within your institution, there are free LMS tools available that can help organize your course, provide a space for you to collect and track grades, give feedback to students, send announcements, place course materials, and so on. In our experience, Google Classroom is one such example of a free LMS that works well as a foundation to organize and set up a virtual classroom.

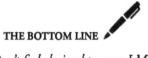

THE BOTTOM LINE

Don't feel chained to your LMS or VC tools. Use the right tool for the outcome or activity of your course.

LMS and Syllabus

The LMS and the syllabus within the LMS can serve as a way to convey to your students the reasons why, the ways you are making use of collaboration, as well as how you will provide feedback to your students both within the LMS and through other tools. Some of the other information that would help learners in the beginning of a virtual course include:

- a list of the tools and software that will be employed throughout the course and why these tools are being used
- links to the tools so students can familiarize themselves with them ahead of time
- contact email and phone number where learners can find information technology support

In Table 1.1, we provide examples of tools we use and information we would provide to our students, so they know how to easily access the tool, the purpose of the tool, the privacy policy, as well as the tool accessibility. Providing this information up front in your course will help learners know what they need and the kinds of tools you will be using in your course. If you are using a tool such as Quality Matters to assess and prepare your course, including a table like Table 1.1 will help ensure your course is meeting a variety of the standards associated with technology tools.

According to the Quality Matters (2020) rubric, standard 6.2 states, "Course tools promote learner engagement and active learning." As you

TABLE 1.1

Sample Tool Description for Students

Name of the Tool	Purpose of the Tool	Privacy Policy	Accessibility
Flipgrid: https://auth.flipgrid.com/signup Note: Sign up as an educator and then invite students to participate in an activity.	• engage learners in discussions that include video, audio, and additions of emojis and other graphic effects • create a sense of community by asking questions that help learners get to know each other • instructor can provide feedback via video/audio and share with learners	https://legal.flipgrid.com/privacy.html	https://help.flipgrid.com/hc/en-us/articles/115004848574-Flipgrid-and-Accessibility
Google Drive: https://www.google.com/drive/ Note: If you do not have a Gmail account, you can create a free Gmail account and then access Google Drive through that account. This will allow you to have access to course materials and resources long after the course ends—this is especially helpful if you are preparing for and studying for content area examinations in the future.	• cloud storage • creating class folders • allows for sharing of assignments and ideas among students and instructors • shared space that can be accessed after the course ends • students can access resources and also add and contribute to class folders	https://policies.google.com/privacy	https://www.google.com/accessibility/

(Continued)

TABLE 1.1 (Continued)

Name of the Tool	Purpose of the Tool	Privacy Policy	Accessibility
Padlet: https://padlet.com/dashboard Note: You do not have to create your own Padlet account if you are adding to the class Padlet—you will just need to double-click on the Padlet to be able to add content, images, text, links, etc.	• digital bulletin board • allows students and instructors to collaborate and share materials and ideas with each other • can be used to share pictures and ask students to introduce themselves to the class • can be used to gather and share materials • can be used as a backchannel for conversation and collaboration	https://padlet.com/about/privacy	https://padlet.com/about/accessibility
VoiceThread: https://voicethread.com/myvoice/ Note: You can create a free VoiceThread account and then you will be able to listen to and comment on any VoiceThread created for this course and shared with you in the course LMS, and you can also create up to 5 free VoiceThread recordings	• embed multimedia that incorporates graphics, texts, figures, and links • provide course content asynchronously • encourage interaction on lectures where students can respond to questions • course discussions with the use of voice and/or video • way for students to collaborate and interact with each other	https://voicethread.com/privacy/	https://voicethread.com/about/features/accessibility

decide on the tools, you will want to consider how your learners are engaged and actively learning. This active learning and engagement can occur synchronously or asynchronously, but you should be able to easily identify that your learners are not passive but actively engaging with the course content, their classmates, and/or you, their instructor.

Standard 6.3 of the Quality Matters (2020) rubric states, "A variety of technology is used in the course." Table 1.1 could help identify the different technologies that are used in the course to meet this standard, and the Purpose of the Tool column can help clarify how the tools are differentiated within a specific course.

Standard 6.4 states, "The course provides learners with information on protecting their data and privacy," and Table 1.1 provides links to all of the privacy statements available for each tool. If a learner is uncomfortable providing their real name on a tool that is not within the course LMS, permission can be granted for them to use a pseudonym and this information can be present within the course LMS and syllabus.

Decisions on Tool Alignment

We use the term *tool,* but this term can also refer to any program or technology you are considering, so we will use the word "tool" to refer to any of these options. Tools have the potential to transform our virtual environments if they are aligned well to our course purpose. We search for tools that are free, easy to use, and easy to implement. When tools are embedded within your course LMS, then typically implementation is easier for both you, your faculty collaborators, and your students. However, this is not always possible or desired, so we encourage you to think about the purpose and utility of the tool you want to use, how it may enhance elements of your course, and what you want your students to learn. We encourage you to try new tools as you go through this book, and we suggest many ways to do this.

Here are a series of recommended steps when deciding on a tool. We frame our discussion of tools around the roles of the virtual instructor. As a faculty member, we know how frustrating it is when we feel we are not getting the support we need, and we also know how isolating our work can be. Finding other faculty members who are trying out tools or can provide support to each other is a great way to gain support unofficially and to learn from others.

We only suggest and discuss tools that fit within accomplishing a particular role in the virtual environment.

THE BOTTOM LINE

We practice what we preach here, so share your ideas in our online shared Google folders: https://tinyurl.com/VISF-folder

Step 1—Focus on Purpose

In this step, we focus on the following questions. What is the purpose of the tool? How will this tool enhance the learning experience, during and after the course? Is the purpose to build community, perform or demonstrate/report learned skills, assess students, increase cognitive presence, social presence, teaching presence? Because we know how important it is to create a community of inquiry as defined by Garrison et al. (2001), we begin with deciding on how this tool/program/technology will help us build a specific presence: a social, cognitive, or teaching presence. Table 1.2 provides examples of what each presence might look like and sample tools you could use to accomplish some of these goals. We discuss the sample tools throughout this book and provide you with reasons to give them a try. Your LMS can provide a basis for establishing social, teaching, and cognitive presence, but you do not have to stop there.

Having decided on the purpose, you can begin evaluating a tool to help you accomplish this goal. Throughout the remaining chapters, we will discuss specific tools, what presence they will help build, their alignment to the previous goals, and why we would choose a particular tool. Although we are only referring specifically to decision-making within this chapter, decision-making will occur throughout your entire role as a virtual instructor.

Step 2—Research the Tool

The next step is to gather more information about the specific tool. After you decide the purpose of the tool and narrow down a few options to use, it is time to do more research. Some questions to consider during this step are as follows:

1. *Will the student have support and access?* When we refer to student support and access, we are referring to whether the student has support if they are having issues with a specific tool and what specific means of access they have. If they only have their cell phone to use as a device, will they still be able to use this tool? Is it embedded within the LMS? If not, how will the students access the tool? Is there a cost to students? Is there training necessary to use the tool? What kind of student support is available? Is there consistency across courses where students use the same tools in different courses? If a tool is not able to be embedded into the LMS, it is

TABLE 1.2
Examples of Social, Teaching, and Cognitive Presence

Social Presence	Teaching Presence	Cognitive Presence
Getting to know other students: Flipgrid https://auth.flipgrid.com/signup	Getting to know the teacher: Prezi https://prezi.com/	Making sense of the content: VoiceThread https://voicethread.com/
Expressing emotions and opinions: LMS discussion board	One-on-one meetings/ conversations with the teacher: Any VC tool	Discussing the content for further understanding: Breakout rooms during live sessions
Creating opportunities for collaboration: Google Drive https://www.google.com/drive/	Asking the teacher questions: Course question discussion board	Digging deeper and taking part in project-based learning, service learning, research
Sharing a story: Powtoon https://www.powtoon.com/account/signup/	Engaging with teacher-directed assignments	Having students respond to other students: Padlet https://padlet.com/dashboard
Building classroom community; supporting each other: Creating an infographic on Canva to share with peers https://www.canva.com/	Introducing a topic or project: Loom https://www.loom.com/	Sharing knowledge and work with each other: Course Google folder
Check-ins: Jamboard https://jamboard.google.com/	Planning and preparing online course for student engagement: Course LMS	Providing peer feedback: Google forms
Creating a sense of belonging: Discussion board through LMS	Creating an environment that is authentic and supportive	Using multimodal modes of instruction—videos, readings, resources: Embedded within LMS

important that the tool is easy to use and that there are links to explain how to use the tool or where to go to find out more about the tool.

2. *Will the tool support your role as instructor and faculty collaboration?* What kind of support and resources are available to the faculty member to use

this tool? Are instructional technology personnel available to support the faculty member? Are funds available to support the faculty member if there are costs associated with the tool? Can this tool be embedded into the LMS? Is there training required?

3. *Does the tool support synchronous and asynchronous instruction?* As a virtual instructor, you will be called on to provide both forms of instruction, and tool usage varies in these two scenarios. How will the tool be used in each one? Some tools work best in an asynchronous environment (learners can interact at different times, allowing for flipped learning and flexibility), while others are best for a synchronous environment (session where learners and teacher are interacting live). Many tools provide flexibility when it comes to how they can be used and can work in both ways. This is information we want to consider before deciding on the best tool. We provide a chapter on synchronous instruction (chapter 4) and asynchronous instruction (chapter 5) that can help guide what method would be best depending on your goal. One of the 10 design principles for a student-centered experience is to allow students to adjust how and when they learn by offering options and formats that can be accessed around their schedules (U.S. Department of Education, 2017).

4. *Does the tool support student-centered ecosystems?* We obviously believe in creating a student-centered ecosystem (U.S. Department of Education, 2017) that supports the changing demographics within our institutions and choosing the right tools can help us do this. Our students can no longer be characterized as they have been in the past. Not all of our undergraduate traditional students can be classified as full-time college students whose only responsibility is to go to school. We can also not assume that our graduate students all fit within the same category or have the same needs. Because of the diversity that exists within our students and the ever-changing demographics in our society, we can help our students succeed best by being aware of these differences, building upon them by providing flexible, stackable options for our students and understanding that a one-size-fits-all approach no longer works. Designing programs, courses, and/or modules around our particular population of students is putting students at the center. Technology can help provide us with opportunities to offer flexibility, accommodations, and accessibility in ways that we could not have done before. So, we suggest keeping this student-centered ecosystem in mind as you evaluate what tool you will use.

Step 3—Document the Decision

To support your own knowledge capture as well as enable sharing and collaboration with other faculty, we created the template Evaluating the Tool (Table 1.3) to guide you as you walk through the steps of deciding on the best tool to use or not to use. Throughout the book, we provide multiple examples of how we use this template and when we decide to use a specific tool. Because there are so many tools to choose from and tools will continue to change, we suggest following this template to help you make an informed choice. The comment section can be used to add notes or questions you have regarding the tool and using it in your specific setting. We provide a QR code to the template for Evaluating the Tool in Figure 1.2. This QR code can be scanned and then you can make a copy of the document and use it yourself as you evaluate tools.

Finding Support After Deciding on a Tool/Strategy

You may be hesitant to try a new tool due to the uncertainty, even with institutional support. Providing faculty with support, time, and resources to make the most of their technology integration is important (Montelongo, 2019). After evaluating the tool and deciding which one to use we suggest reflecting on the following questions:

- Where can I go to find resources to support my efforts?
- How can I obtain the training I need?
- How comfortable am I with taking a risk and trying something new?
- How can I find ways to collaborate with other faculty and administration?

Our research indicates that faculty need time to collaborate with colleagues, share ideas, and explore virtual learning in a supportive environment. Sometimes in institutions, this culture of transparency, collaboration, and sharing may need to be cultivated and developed. We found this out in 2020 during the pandemic when virtual teaching was something most faculty had to do with no warning and many with little to no support. Faculty learned to rely on each other to make decisions on how to engage their learners and become facilitators and decision makers in their virtual environments. Many learned through social media and trial and error when the world suddenly changed.

The top skill faculty reported as developing during this stressful time was flexibility. One group of experts concluded the need for flexibility during virtual learning was based on the evaluation of the learner, the

TABLE 1.3
Evaluating the Tool Template

Name of Tool	Building Social Presence (list how)	Building Teaching Presence (list how)	Building Cognitive Presence (list how)	Tool is embedded in the LMS or has capability to be embedded into the LMS (Yes or No)	Format: Asynchronous Synchronous Face-to-Face Dual Learner
Comments					
Questions to Consider					
What role are you fulfilling as a virtual instructor?					
What organizational resources do you need to implement this tool?					
What support do you need to use the tool besides an internet connection?					
What is your backup plan if the tool does not work or does not accomplish what you thought it would?					

FACULTY PERSPECTIVES

One faculty member stated when asked about teaching virtually in 2020–2021, "there was less content covered, but all involved built skills and tool sets that will serve all of us well going forward."

Another shared the following: "There were a lot of resources provided, but difficult to implement due to the learning curve and extent of other responsibilities. Implementation was like a second full-time job, with no real support on that process."

tasks the learner would perform, the tools used, and the context in which the learning took place (Rapanta et al., 2020). In our follow-up survey, faculty indicated a variety of skills they developed due to teaching in 2020–2021, and flexibility was one of the greatest skills noted. The identification of the many skills faculties developed also aligns with the research stating that faculty need practice in developing skills such as creativity, innovation, flexibility, and so on (Mehta et al., 2019). Although this was a challenging time for most faculty and students, our research highlights that it was also a time of growth and learning.

Virtual learning, if done well, should provide a level of flexibility to both faculty and students. With the multitude of pressures within our society we face while balancing teaching, learning, and life responsibilities such as work and family, flexibility may be the only way someone can pursue their education or career aspirations. Virtual learning that is flexible can also increase access across diverse populations, engage learners in deeper learning, and allow for challenges that may arise in life.

Virtual Instructor as a Facilitator/Coach

From surveying faculty, we believe one of the hardest changes to make is moving from a teacher-centered role to a more student-centered role in a virtual environment. Because the virtual environment allows for flexibility and does not necessarily have a specified amount of time where students will be in front of their instructors, it can seem overwhelming when self-assessing and reflecting upon our teaching. We use tools like the OLC scorecards (2016) to help us self-assess our virtual instruction and ensure that we are continually improving and setting up a positive learning environment for our students. We provide a QR code (Figure 1.4) to the site where you can find these free templates. We have found the Quality Course Teaching and Instructional Practice template from the OLC to be helpful when self-assessing the engagement in our virtual teaching. We suggest that you download these free scorecards and use them as you work through this book.

When reflecting on the role of the instructor as a facilitator/coach, we use the following points to help guide our reflection:

- *Build teaching presence*: Instructor is present in the course and the course is ready and set up for the learners. Learners are able to seek help if they have questions and the instructor responds in a timely manner to help clarify and connect with learners.
- *Create a flexible and responsive environment*: Instructor is flexible and responsive to student needs. If necessary, the course is revised and made clearer per student questions, and these updates are communicated to the learners via the course LMS announcements, emails, and/or in live synchronous sessions.
- *Encourage and support self-directed learning*: Instructor sets the course up so learners can be self-directed and move through the course with ease. Strategies that encourage students to be self-directed and take responsibility for their learning are embedded within the course. Instructors scaffold and provide announcements via the course LMS and meet one-on-one with learners who may be having difficulty navigating within the virtual environment.

- *Clarify role as facilitator.* Because learners may not be familiar with the role of the faculty member as a facilitator in the virtual environment, we suggest explaining this in the beginning of the course via an introduction video (Screencastify or Loom) and/or having this explanation included in the syllabus (which is now embedded within the LMS and the course).

Faculty Perspectives

We surveyed and worked with many faculty members while doing this research and working on this book. We want to highlight their perspectives, desires, thoughts, and ideas throughout this book. We wrote this book to be a support and a guide as they continue to create engaging virtual environments. When asked what kind of supports faculty needed when we surveyed them in the fall of 2020, here is a sampling of faculty responses:

- There were a lot of resources provided, but difficult to implement due to the learning curve and extent of other responsibilities. Implementation was like a second full-time job, with no real support on that process.
- More of the basics for faculty who were not comfortable/stressed by the shift.
- Regular suggestions on where to refer students for additional help with assignments. Suggestions on how to engage unresponsive students in virtual settings.
- It is difficult to always know what the students are doing off-screen. My concern is that they are wandering. I do not think there's support for it but that has been a concern.

We know faculty need support as much as their students need support. From the many comments we received, we believe faculty will benefit from practical suggestions, ideas, and time to help them make decisions about tools they will use, course design, and ways to facilitate/coach their students toward learning. We know how important it is for faculty to know their students are engaged and learning. In the next section, we discuss mindsets that support decision-making and facilitation of virtual instruction.

Mindsets to Support Decision-Making and Facilitation of Virtual Instruction

As transformative as technology can be, we know that it can also be frustrating at times. Things may not work the way we plan them to work and instead of looking at these situations as negative, we can look at them as an opportunity to develop the mindsets that support us in our virtual instruction endeavors. The top tier of mindsets developed by faculty surveyed during the 2020–2021 academic year included *flexibility, innovation, problem-solving, creativity,* and *open-mindedness.*

These are the same mindsets we want to help our learners develop. The second tier of mindsets developed consisted of *collaboration, time management, being comfortable with ambiguity,* and *the willingness to take risks.* The third tier included the *ability to differentiate* and to be *willing to play.* These mindsets help us to confront problems, make decisions, become facilitators and coaches within our virtual environments, try new tools and ways of teaching, think critically and creatively about ways to solve problems we encounter during virtual instruction, and to keep persisting even when things are difficult.

FACULTY PERSPECTIVES

These faculty quotes demonstrate the growth and the positive mindsets that came from challenging times during 2020–2021 teaching:

"We are learning to be adaptive."

"Having to rethink how to do things. It is forcing me to change things up from what I usually do."

"I get to learn new things and see where my past teaching could improve."

Faculty can model to learners by being open and honest about challenges and asking for feedback regarding the teaching and learning that is taking place. The role of the faculty member changes in virtual instruction to one of a facilitator who supports and guides learning by setting up the environment where learners can learn from the content, the instructor, and each other.

Developing Mindsets to Support Virtual Learning

Mehta et al. (2019) assessed that faculty need time to practice and discuss the mindsets that will support their virtual teaching and learning. Being more aware of the mindsets that will help us thrive in virtual environments can help us develop these skills and to intentionally practice them. The only way to get better at these mindsets that support virtual teaching and learning is to be intentional about building these skills and work with others in identifying where they see these skills in practice and what they look like in a virtual environment. This can happen by learning them directly or by seeing them performed by others and talking about situations and scenarios that might reflect on these mindsets. In chapter 3, we will discuss the benefit of having a team and how the practice of sharing, coconstructing knowledge, and working with others will reinforce learning and internalize these mindsets.

We suggest that you pick one or more of the mindsets that support teaching and learning in a virtual environment (examples: creativity, flexibility, problem-solving, etc.) and find a partner to discuss this skill with. You can use a template like the one in Table 1.4 to complete and share ideas with your partner or reflect on your own experiences if you wanted to use this chart by yourself. In the first column, you would list the mindset you are discussing, in the second column, share an idea of where you saw this mindset being displayed, and the third column lists ways you can practice this mindset.

Part 2: Tips, Tools, and Templates to Support the Virtual Instructor as Decision Maker and Facilitator

Our suggestions can be modified to work in different settings and not everything we suggest will work for you in your environment. This is okay—use what you can, share with a friend, and/or send us your own ideas as we hope to build on everything we discuss in this book and collaborate with all of you as we build a shared space for continued learning, which we will discuss further in chapter 7.

Tips

As facilitators of learning in a virtual environment, we need to remember that many students are taking their courses in an online environment to integrate their studies with their life and work schedules, driving a specific focus of being flexible and responsive to our students' needs. We suggest a variety of examples on how to create this flexible environment as a facilitator and coach of virtual instruction and how to support our students as self-directed learners.

Creating a Flexible, Responsive Virtual Environment

- Use a screencasting tool to quickly record your screen, answer questions that a student may have, and provide directions on how to use a tool or to clarify a course assignment or activity (example tools such as Loom or Screencastify).
- Create a short video using your cell phone and then upload video to YouTube to share with students.

TABLE 1.4
Mindsets That Support Virtual Instruction

Mindsets	Where did you see this demonstrated during virtual instruction either by yourself, a colleague, or a student?	What are some things you can do to build this skill?
Flexibility	I saw that my students were overwhelmed with life, and they needed flexibility when it came to due dates. They appreciated having extra time to complete assignments and I appreciated that they were communicating with me.	Start by checking in more often on the well-being of students and others and letting them know I am thinking of them and am able to be flexible if needed.
Problem-Solving	I had a student who could not be part of a group project due to personal issues, so I allowed them to do a project off of a book they were currently reading for work that was related to the course.	Stay calm when a problem arises and focus on student learning and how solving the problem can help with students' learning.
Collaboration	I was part of a strategic planning group where our goal was to see what kind of support was available to faculty when it came to virtual learning. I enjoyed collaborating with the other faculty members and sharing ideas with them on how to create more engaging learning environments.	Find someone new to work with that I have not worked with before—decide to try a new virtual tool together or offer to do a virtual walk of their classroom and offer feedback and ask for them to do the same in my virtual classroom.

- Sign up to use Google Voice to obtain a number to share with your students so they can get in touch with you (without having to give your personal cell phone).
- Use the announcement section of your LMS to share messages with your students and answer questions that even one student had but others may also have but have not asked yet.
- Invite students to set up virtual meetings with you one-on-one to share concerns or ask questions. This also builds teaching presence when students have opportunities to meet individually with their instructors.

Strategies to Help Students Become Self-Directed Learners

- Allow students to choose their content area (hopefully something they are passionate about) for a project.
- Encourage students to collaborate and share their learning with their peers. Sharing assignments via a shared class folder within Google Drive can provide an easy way for collaboration to take place and for students to be self-directed. We recommend setting this up in the beginning of the course and explaining the idea of sharing ideas and collaborating with their classmates throughout the course. This helps develop self-directed learners because students can see examples of other students' work and past student work (if applicable) and they can use these ideas to help them with their own work. Self-directed learners learn with and through each other.
- Within the course LMS, provide information related to all projects within the course, even the final project, and encourage learners to work on their projects from the beginning of the course at their own pace. Allowing students to choose the content area they will focus on, or other aspects of their project, can also help encourage self-directed learning.
- Set up a common area where student work can be submitted and shared. This could also be within a shared class folder where all assignments are submitted. This way students can see not only their own work but their classmates' work.
- Engage students in peer review and providing feedback to their peers on their work. This can be done using a tool like Google Forms or even on a Padlet page where students can share links to their work and then comment directly on the Padlet to each other.

Tools

Loom—Screencasting Tool to Increase Engagement and Communicate With Students

As mentioned earlier in this chapter, Loom is a screencasting tool to use to provide quick clarification and directions to students. Students can also use Loom to communicate with you and their classmates about something they want to demonstrate or explain. There is a 5-minute limit for the free version, but this is usually a perfect amount of time to send out messages or explanations to students.

Figure 1.1. Demonstration of how Loom can be used to introduce students to your virtual course.

An example of a short Loom video created to introduce students to the virtual course and to get them started can be found at https://tinyurl.com/Loom-VISF or scan the QR code in Figure 1.1.

Templates

QR Code for Evaluating the Tool Template

The Evaluating the Tool template can be used to help you make decisions about the tool you want to use. Feel free to scan this QR code (Figure 1.2) and copy this template, modify it if needed, and use it to help determine if the tool you are considering will help you meet your teaching and learning goals and support student learning in a virtual environment.

QR Code for Mindsets to Support Virtual Teaching and Learning Activity Template

You can scan this QR code (Figure 1.3), copy the template, and use this activity to help you discuss the mindsets you are developing or would like to develop within your virtual teaching and learning. Sometimes having a conversation with another faculty member and realizing you are not alone can greatly help and this activity can be a conversation starter.

QR Code for the Free OLC Scorecards

The OLC (2016) scorecards provide an excellent way to self-assess your virtual teaching and learning. The scorecards are free to download and easy to use and we encourage you to scan the QR code (Figure 1.4) and download the scorecards and use them either individually or within learning communities to help you as you improve your virtual courses.

Figure 1.2. Scan this QR code to have access to the Evaluating the Tool template described in Table 1.2.

Figure 1.3. The Mindsets to Support Virtual Instruction activity described in Table 1.4 can be completed by scanning this QR code and making a copy of the template for your use either individually or with others.

Figure 1.4. Link to the OLC scorecards where you can download them and use them to help self-assess your virtual teaching.

Wrapping It Up

In this chapter, we provide tools that you can use right away and a framework to guide your virtual teaching and learning in the role of virtual instructor as decision maker and facilitator/coach. We wrap up this section with the following key points:

- Your role as a virtual instructor shifts in a virtual environment to a facilitator of teaching and learning. You will want to find opportunities to create teaching presence, cognitive presence, and social presence and ensure that your learners are self-directed learners and understand the shift in roles present within the virtual classroom.
- As a decision maker, you will have many opportunities to choose tools and ways for your students to learn. Be sure to focus not on the tool, but on the learning, and use the tools to help accomplish these goals.
- There are shared resources we use to guide our decisions and facilitation of virtual instruction such as the Evaluating the Tool template and the Mindsets That Support Virtual Instruction activity. Use these tools to guide and support your decisions and facilitation in your virtual environments.
- Embrace flexibility and the mindsets discussed within this chapter. Give yourself a break and try to have fun while creating engaging, flexible environments for your learners and yourself. We know how important it is to develop mindsets that embrace the unknowns that come with teaching in a virtual environment.

In the following chapter, we will focus on building community within a virtual environment, and we provide many ways to do this by personalizing your course, checking in with your students using virtual tools, and building social presence.

Chapter 1 Reflection Questions

1. What kind of mindsets have you developed or hope to develop from virtual teaching and learning?
2. What are some ways you have or can create a flexible, responsive environment?
3. How do you help your students become self-directed learners in a virtual environment?
4. What examples can you add to Table 1.1 of ways that you create social, teaching, and cognitive presence in your virtual classroom?

VIRTUAL INSTRUCTOR AS A COMMUNITY BUILDER AND SUPPORTER

Please mute your mic.

—A quote used by every teacher in 2020

This chapter focuses on providing tips, tools, and templates on how to create a space that is positive for social emotional learning, which will include check-ins with our students. We suggest strategies we use on ensuring students feel welcome when they enter their virtual environment and building connections with students. We suggest using tools like Padlet, Jamboard, Canva, and so on to establish this type of connection and enhance your virtual classroom. We also believe that the use of humor is important to building connections with our students.

Part 1: Describing the Role of Virtual Instructor as a Community Builder and Supporter

We will define the roles of a virtual instructor as a community builder and supporter to ensure we are providing clarity on how we approach this important role. We first need to understand what the role is before we can proceed on how to become this role in the virtual classroom. Our responsibility as an instructor in the virtual classroom is to provide a safe space for all our learners and to be all inclusive and to support our learners throughout the course. Usually when teachers talk about ensuring all students feel safe and supported, we focus on what happens in a physical classroom. But in this chapter, we will focus on how we set up a safe virtual environment because this setting can be stressful and scary for many students. As instructors, we want to make our students feel safe, and we also want to consider how we are going to support their well-being and mental health.

THE BOTTOM LINE

Provide a safe space for learners.

Defining the Role of Virtual Instructor as a Community Builder and Supporter

We define the *role of a virtual instructor as a community builder and supporter* as an instructor who will create an atmosphere in a virtual setting that teaches students that they are valued and connected to the instructor and other students in the class, and to help nurture students' feelings of accountability. Defining this role as a community builder, instructors will be creating a virtual environment where students will work together as a class toward the shared goal of learning, to feel safe to respond freely and to ask questions all throughout the sessions, in addition to the instructor providing the support to students to have them reach their fullest potential. This type of environment will teach students the importance of collaborating with one another, as well as supporting social and emotional skills in a virtual environment, and help learners develop a sense of responsibility toward others. To provide this safe environment for our learners, we need to set the stage first and establish the norms of a virtual community.

Establishing the Communication Norms of the Virtual Classroom

What exactly is establishing the norms? What are the norms of a virtual classroom? We need to realize that although many of our students might spend much of their personal time on some type of online device and on some type of social media, they might not have the skill sets necessary to communicate in a virtual classroom setting. So, instructors in this role of a community builder, we must set the expectations for students for communicating in this virtual academic environment. On the first day of the semester, we suggest doing an activity to get students' input on the dos and don'ts of online communication, which often resonates with them and is relatable since they are the ones creating the lists. This approach is much more effective than just distributing a list

GREAT IDEA!

On the first day of the semester, have students create a dos and don'ts list of online communication.

of guidelines; students feel included when they can create their own list of agreed-upon online behaviors.

Once the norms for online communication have been established, you now can begin to build community and support the learners through the various tips, tools, and templates that will be discussed throughout this chapter. We will focus on how we should do icebreakers, do check-ins with our students, as well as create a space that is positive for social-emotional learning. We will ask students to share their ideas and take academic risks during class, so in this role of *community builder and supporter*, we need to make sure that we have created a safe space that fosters interactions between instructor and student as well as student to student. Students want a strong connection with their professors, and developing this connection is critically important to students. It generally fuels their excitement to learn when they have a connection to their professor through formal and informal interactions and communication. So, we will suggest tools to use like Padlet, Jamboard, Canva, and so on to establish this type of connection, and to enhance your virtual classroom. Additionally, humor is touched on and how you can add it to your virtual environment.

Designing remote learning for students is not the same as copying in-person instruction into Canvas or any other LMS; however, many of the same principles apply. But first, we must start with building relationships with our students before the learning can begin. How do you do that, you ask? Well, there are many ways of creating a safe social-emotional space for students in a virtual classroom. If we build these crucial, strong social-emotional connections, this will motivate students to remain respectful and supportive and follow their own rules in the virtual classroom.

THE BOTTOM LINE

Build relationships with students.

What is it like when you first enter a virtual classroom, or a meeting for that matter? Do you sit there with your camera on, asking yourself if you should keep it on, or what should you be doing before the class/meeting begins? Do you sit there in silence just looking uncomfortably with others on the screen? Well, this is one of the reasons we suggest using what they call a "landing page" when the students first get into your virtual class, which is a visual of what your class will cover as well as welcoming them to class. And to address the uncomfortable silence, you can have music playing in the background. This chapter will focus on creating a safe and welcoming virtual space and ways we do this in our own virtual classrooms by creating a landing page, changing virtual backgrounds, building community, and integrating music in the background.

Building Community

As educators, we know that building community in a virtual environment increases the likelihood of student success, in not only their grades, but also in their social-emotional development. Building community and a safe space is based on trust and respect, and that often begins with the relationship between student and teacher. It is important to build this trust in a virtual environment and foster these relationships. However, finding ways to make them feel like they belong can be difficult. Students often feel isolated in online courses because the teacher did not make them feel like they cared about them. Research has shown that the course's level of interpersonal inter-action is the most important factor in predicting a student's grade in an online course (Jaggars et al., 2013). So, knowing how important these interactions are, how do we go about building community in our virtual classroom?

As stated in chapter 1, we need to focus on purpose and what tool/program/technology will help us build a specific presence. In this chapter we will be focusing on teaching, social, and cognitive presences (italicized items in Table 2.1), and keeping these items in mind:

TABLE 2.1
Examples of Social, Teaching, and Cognitive Presence

Social Presence	Teaching Presence	Cognitive Presence
Getting to know other students	*Getting to know the teacher*	Making sense of the content
Expressing emotions and opinions	One-on-one meetings/conversations with the teacher	Discussing the content for further understanding
Creating opportunities for collaboration	*Asking the teacher questions*	*Digging deeper and taking part in project-based learning, service learning, research*
Sharing a story	*Engaging with teacher-directed assignments*	*Having students respond to other students*
Building classroom community; supporting each other	*Introducing a topic or project*	*Sharing knowledge and work with each other*
Check-ins	*Planning and preparing online course for student engagement*	*Providing peer feedback*
Creating a sense of belonging	*Create an environment that is authentic and supportive*	*Using multimodal modes of instruction—videos, readings, resources*

Personalize Your Course

To start, we suggest personalizing your course in both your LMS (Canvas, Blackboard, etc.) and in your synchronous and asynchronous sessions. Personalize your course wherever possible because your online learners need to feel the presence of their instructor and fellow students. You can promote your students' sense of you (social presence) and your teaching presence as an authentic person in the online classroom.

GREAT IDEA!

Create a page in your LMS that describes YOU!

To create this sense of social presence, a technique that helps students feel connected is a page that describes you and your background and interests and includes your photo. There are many templates available to choose from that are free, but we purchased a layout from Teachers Pay Teachers (scan QR code in Figure 2.1 to access) which is a great website to purchase items for teaching. Here is an example in Figure 2.2 of the "Meet the Teacher" document that is provided in the LMS for the students to view any time during the semester. There are many templates to choose from, and you can find one most aligned to your discipline.

Including a picture of yourself helps students make connections with you, but another great suggestion is to ask students to include photos and profiles too. This can add to the social presence; however, some students might not like their picture or information shared. So, you could ask them to post pet pictures instead and add some information about them and why they selected this as their profile picture.

Figure 2.1. Scan QR code to access Teachers Pay Teachers.

Figure 2.2. Example of Meet the Teacher document shared in virtual classroom.

Create a Movie Trailer/Video to Welcome Students to Your Class

Additionally, we created an iMovie of what the class was going to be about using the trailer feature. (See Figure 2.3.) This is also in the LMS for students to view before the semester begins. We created the video and then uploaded it to YouTube for free. When you upload to YouTube, you are provided a link that you can copy and share with your students and embed into your LMS "About the Class" page. For the iMovie, you can make use of your Bitmoji, but for copyright purposes, we cannot include ours in this publication. A video clip could contain exciting course content and assignments, but it is

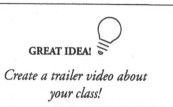

GREAT IDEA!

Create a trailer video about your class!

solely intended to make students feel welcome and connected. Here is the link to the YouTube video Welcome back to ECE (https://tinyurl.com/VISF-ece) and we provide a QR Code to scan in Figure 2.4.

Figure 2.3. Screenshot of movie trailer welcoming students to class.

Figure 2.4. Scan QR code to access YouTube welcome video example.

Figure 2.5. Scan QR code to access Office of Instructional Success example video.

After creating one trailer video, it is easy to make them for each one of your courses. We also created ones for the Early Childhood Department, each course that we teach, as well as for the Office of Instructional Success (https://tinyurl.com/VISF-OIS or scan the QR code provided in Figure 2.5). Here are the steps to creating a trailer video using iMovie. If you do not have an iPhone, there are many video apps available that you can use to create a trailer like the iMovie.

Create a Communication Plan

Communication is key in any relationship, so the one you create with your students should be no different. Creating a plan for communication is a great way to reinforce the ways you will be available to them, as well as how they will be able to get in touch with you.

Announcements in Your LMS

In your LMS, there should be an announcement function, where you are able to send the whole class an announcement. We use our Bitmojis for everything because they are currently very trendy, and students like them and can relate to them. It is easy to get your Bitmoji embedded into your email and on your toolbar. Bitmojis are an easy way to create a fun virtual avatar of yourself and use it with your students.

BIG IDEA!

Communication is key in any relationship!

Before the first week of the semester, send an announcement to the whole class explaining that they should access your course in the LMS and look at the course module, which will explain what the course is about as well as your "Meet the Teacher" document and possibly video trailer. You should also include information on how students can get in touch with you by providing your number and email address and when it is best to reach out to you or meet during office hours.

Additionally, make use of the announcement function to send messages before the next class of what is due and what to expect for the next session. It is also beneficial to send a message to the whole class after a session if they performed well on a presentation or were highly engaged in the class. It encourages the students to continue to do so in future classes.

> **GREAT IDEA!**
>
> *Send messages to students in your LMS each week!*

Encourage Engagement

Interaction in a virtual environment is far more difficult than in a face-to-face classroom. As the instructor, you need to be more deliberate about your student–student and student–teacher interactions. Depending on whether your class is asynchronous or synchronous, you can make use of discussion boards, group projects, chat boxes, and virtual programs like Jamboard and Padlet.

As a way to be sure that every student in your class is participating, you can make use of an online name generator. You can share your screen and show the wheel with everyone's name on it. Then virtually spin the wheel and a name is generated, and then it would be that student's turn to participate. Using a name generator not only eliminates teacher bias when calling on students, but it also increases participation, discussion, and focus in class.

Creating a Landing Page

Before you figure out what should be on a landing page, let us discuss why we use landing pages. Landing pages are primarily used on websites by companies, and the main purpose of a landing page is to encourage visitors to act, to warm up potential customers to a product, and to provide further information. If we use that same mindset with our students, we want our students to look at the items on the landing page and act, especially if we are requesting them to scan a QR code or to visit a website. We also are trying to warm up our students by having them read the agenda and the objectives of the class, so they know what they can expect from that class session. But it also is a nice screen to view before class starts and engage students as they are logging onto the session.

Benefits of Using a Landing Page

The following is an example of a landing page using the website class-roomscreen.com, but there are other tools you can use to create the same scene. This screen is shown by sharing your screen like you do with PowerPoint. We provide an example in our Supplemental Resource folder and a QR code to go right to the document in the folder in Figure 2.6. The example is from an Early Childhood Education class, so when students log onto their virtual class, they would see a landing page that helps them get started and ready for the synchronous session.

GREAT IDEA!

Create a landing page for students to view before class begins!

As you can see, there is a lot of information shown on the screen that the students will be able to read while they log in and are waiting for class to begin. Often there are QR codes they can scan and access before class begins as well. This screen can also be shown at the end of class to summarize the main ideas, highlight upcoming assignments, and show how all of these connect to the next session and how to prepare for it.

Figure 2.6. Scan QR code to see an example of a landing page used to begin a virtual synchronous session.

Student Perspectives

We asked students what they thought of the landing pages we used during our live synchronous sessions. Their perspectives are highlighted below.

STUDENT PERSPECTIVES

Yes. This was a great addition to online learning. I found myself wanting it in other classes where professors did not use it.

Yes, it helped because I knew what was expected of me.

Yes, because it was a clear overview of what the whole class was going to be about.

Yes, because it shows me what is expected in each class, and it was very fun and creative to look at.

What Should Be on a Landing Page?

As you can see in Figure 2.7, there are many items included on the landing page for this class. We always include certain items that we think are important for the students to see when they first enter the virtual class. We make use of our logo as a center point of the page, as well as the agenda. Included on the page are reminders of assignments that are due or coming up, what tools they need to have readily available for the virtual class, the date, a quote, and the class countdown (which is live when you click Play). More information on the countdown clock will be provided later because it is a tool we use to count down before class begins as well as when they are on break. And speaking of break, we also include on the agenda break time so that students can plan around that. Not seen on this screenshot are QR codes. We would often provide QR codes to items that we wanted students to access during class if they wanted to use their phones in addition to their laptops. Everything you see on this screenshot are the items that we found useful; however, you might find other items more important for students to see and access while they are waiting for your class to begin.

Figure 2.7. Identifies the various icons available on a landing page in classroomscreen.com.

     Quote

Logo   Agenda   Calendar   Tools   Reminders   Quote   Timer

Background Music in Virtual Classroom

Another idea to welcome your students to your virtual classroom is to have background music playing as they enter your class (combined with the landing page). Music eliminates the "dead air" that is there before class begins, plus the students like hearing music. You can pick music that goes along with the theme of your class, or something that you might think the students would enjoy hearing.

Soft background music in a virtual classroom can help support focus and learning in the students. A great way to involve your students in the music selection is to have each student provide you with their favorite song that you will add to a playlist. Then randomly play your playlist at the beginning of each class, as well as during break time. Students get very excited when they hear "their song."

Background music can also be played while students are actively engaged in an online activity. We often would play acoustic pop music during this time, and if you observe your students, you will notice that they are happy and more productive when they can hear the background music. It is a stress reducer, and students seem to enjoy listening to it while they are involved with individual activities. We selected pop acoustic music because the students could relate and sometimes sing along to the music that they were hearing.

Checking In With Students

Now that you have created your landing page and have background music playing for your students before class begins, you are ready to start class. The best way to begin any class is to have a check-in with your students to see how they are doing. It is easier to cultivate social connection and build community in the virtual classroom when you begin each class with an icebreaker activity or opening check-in. This is unrelated to coursework; you are simply gauging how they are doing. We know through research that students want a teacher who cares about them in and out of the classroom. As instructors, we need to build these positive relationships that are intentional and inclusive of everyone in the class.

A simple check-in with our students builds rapport and trust and shows the students that we are intentionally trying to connect to each of them. These simple check-ins can focus on students' wellness,

BIG IDEA!

A simple check-in helps build rapport with students!

their emotional status, and their social connectedness. You can even give a simple hello to each student in the class as they enter the virtual classroom (if it is a relatively small class). It is suggested that you do not cover any content in those first 5–10 minutes of class, and just check in with students and find out how they are doing. Social-emotional learning is a top priority in a virtual classroom since you do not physically see them. These check-ins and questions send the message to the students that you care about them, and you want to know how they are doing. Frequent check-ins make students feel known and understood, even when they are taking a class at a distance.

Types of Virtual Check-Ins

Social-emotional learning plays a critical role in our virtual classrooms, as we take on the role of virtual instructor as a supporter. It is imperative to integrate these learning opportunities into your virtual classroom so that students can develop their own voice and have a sense of belonging. As educators, we need to add opportunities for our students to identify things during class such as self-awareness, social awareness, and self-management. Students should be encouraged to become more aware of how they are feeling, and how they can express themselves in an appropriate way. Students need these opportunities to develop these skills during your virtual class to benefit their well-being as well as their learning.

Social-Emotional Pulse Check

A quick way to check in with students without using technology is to use "cheers and jeers" to begin a class as a warm-up activity. Students are invited and encouraged to tell the class anything positive that happened to them over the past week, no matter how small. It is amazing what students will tell the class, as well as which students volunteer!

Another way to say hello is to say hello to each student by name (if this is feasible), and if they do not want to unmute themselves, tell them to just wave. When they hear their name, they usually just smile and wave. This is another reason to request students to have their cameras on during class.

Student Perspectives

We asked our students what their thoughts were about the check-ins that we inserted into our synchronous and asynchronous sessions, and they responded favorably. Their responses are highlighted on p. 49.

Using Scale Images or Emojis to Check In

You can create a document that you share on your screen that asks the students how they are doing, and then the students would use specific tools to respond. One document you could create and share would be one of a scale with features that students would be able to use within a video conferencing tool, like Zoom, where they could "write" their rating using images, emojis, x marks, and so forth. There are many scales you can find and use from the internet if you do a basic search of "how are you doing scale image." You can find one that is appropriate for your class; however, we suggest using something funny that students can relate to like pictures of dogs' or cats' faces. Many of these images are subject to copyright, so they are not shown as an example in the book, but you can use them if you copy and paste from the internet. We share an example of one we created using PowerPoint and the Design Ideas function (Figure 2.8).

STUDENT PERSPECTIVES

I liked doing the check-ins because I like knowing that my teachers care about how I am feeling and that means a lot to me because other teachers do not ask you that.

Yes, because it is always good to start; kind of like breaking the ice. It gives me some time to wake up and get ready.

Yes, because it shows me that our professor cares about us and wants to know how we are doing physically and mentally.

Surveys

Surveys are an easy, private way to check in with students. To build those teacher–student relationships as well as strengthen their social-emotional health, surveys provide that opportunity for each student. When used during

Figure 2.8. An example of a check-in we created using PowerPoint and the Design Idea function.

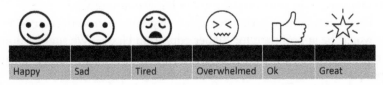

a synchronous session, students will participate in real time, and you will be able to see their responses once they click the submit button. The survey could ask questions about what their experiences were like for that class or perhaps the one prior to that. Surveys tend to center on student course experience, but you should also include a few questions that deal with social-emotional learning and their well-being. Be sure to limit the number of questions on a survey to avoid survey fatigue; you might want to limit the survey to three to five questions.

Polling

Polling is a simple way to gauge how students are feeling by asking them a series of questions and then they respond accordingly in real time. Polls offer immediate, real-time feedback that can gauge how students are doing both with the class as well as socially-emotionally. Polls offer a quick and accurate low-stakes way for students to respond and for you to assess your audience. Since it is a low-stakes activity, this will help naturally shy or introverted students to participate.

Additionally, polls featuring an open-ended question often serve as a starting point for discussion to begin class. Polls serve as a launching point for the class, and since they are anonymous, students can freely answer questions. There are many free polling platforms available, including Mentimeter, for which a link is provided for you at the end of this chapter.

BIG IDEA!

Polling is an easy way to check in with students!

Social-Emotional Learning

Introductions (in Beginning of Semester)

Icebreakers are commonly used to encourage students to participate and have conversations with each other and you. They are done to create a relaxed environment at the beginning of the semester to help students feel comfortable in your virtual classroom. As the instructor, you will facilitate an icebreaker and help your students get to know one another.

There are many websites that offer suggestions on icebreaker activities that would be appropriate for higher education classes. We suggest doing a Google search on icebreakers or look on Pinterest, but one that is culturally responsive is called The Story of Your Name.

Story of Your Name

The purpose of this activity is to get to know everyone's name but done with each person telling the story of their name to the class. The instructor would invite each student to tell a story about any part of their name.

GREAT IDEA!

As an icebreaker, have students tell the story of their name!

It could be their first name, last name, middle name, married name, or nickname. Tell each student that they can share as much or as little as makes them comfortable. Depending on the class size, you can facilitate it as a whole group exercise or put them into breakout groups and let them share with each other. It is suggested that you have a timer so that each student has 2 minutes to share their name story.

We did this activity many times and the students seem to enjoy it more than the typical icebreakers of introductions. This also is a great activity to emphasize diversity in the classroom, and students get to learn something about their classmates that they might not have otherwise.

If students are struggling to explain their story, you might want to pose some questions to spark some ideas, such as:

- How was this name chosen? And by whom?
- Were you named after someone?
- Does your name have any cultural significance or historical meaning?
- Is there a story behind how you were named that you would like to share?

Course Reflections

Course reflections are personal surveys that you can send out to your students at the end of the semester for you to get feedback on how you did for the semester. This is not the same as the course evaluations that students do each semester for every professor. Course reflections would be created by you, and you would ask questions that would provide feedback so that you could improve your course each semester. This could be an informal document that you type up with questions to which students would type their answers during the last class and submit via email or upload into your LMS or create something like a Google Form and provide the students with a link.

Word of caution: you might get some responses that are not quite favorable, but sometimes it is these comments that make the most impact! It is okay to make yourself vulnerable and ask them questions that might result in unfavorable answers; those comments are the ones where you need to make a change to your practice. If most of your students respond a certain way, then we suggest reflecting on how to make a change. If it is only a few, then maybe accept their responses and try to make accommodations to what they said.

On the flip side, you might get wonderful feedback with lots of positive responses! This is promising, especially if you ask them to rate how a new activity or assessment was during the semester. These are just as impactful because you can continue to do these activities and assessments in the next semester. Let students express their thoughts, feelings, and emotions. Ask them to be perfectly honest in their responses because their answers will not affect their grade whatsoever. Examples of the questions will be found in Part 2: Tips.

Student Perspectives

Many of the student perspectives we share within our book come from course reflections that we had in our courses. We particularly like to reflect on student responses related to something positive they liked within our course.

Thank a Classmate

Are students ever offered an opportunity to thank a classmate for helping them during the semester? As the semester winds down and the natural practice of reflection begins, it should be encouraged that the students take the time to thank their classmate(s) who have helped them during the semester. What better way to acknowledge those students who help others in the class by giving everyone an opportunity to thank a classmate.

> ### STUDENT PERSPECTIVES
>
> *Really good with making each Zoom class not boring*
>
> *Professor Ricevuto always includes other types of technology into the class that makes it interesting.*
>
> *Virtual learning has been tough on everyone, but I always look forward to my Wednesday class because Dr. Ricevuto makes it fun.*
>
> *She uses a Jamboard to ask how we are feeling.*
>
> *Dr. Ricevuto gives positive feedback on all assignments through Canvas and through messages. I do not usually see other professors do this, but she did it in both semesters and I love how she uplifts her students.*

One way to offer this opportunity is to house a "Thank a Classmate" page in your LMS. Once students access the page, there should be a link to a

Google Form (or whatever platform you use) that they would complete on which classmate(s) they would like to thank. Once students access the form, this is a suggestion of what it could say:

GREAT IDEA!

Give students the opportunity to thank one of their classmates for helping them during the semester!

> Please use this form to recognize your classmates' unseen work in this course with 1–2 extra credit points. If your classmates have helped you understand concepts, feel comfortable in class, or complete assignments, please indicate how they helped you, and suggest how many points you think this action deserves. Actions that can be recognized include but are not limited to: offering feedback on your work, sharing notes, posing good questions, making helpful jokes, offering emotional support, or otherwise helping.

Students can opt to be anonymous, or they can choose to let the student know that they are nominating them and that they submitted the form to thank them.

Part 2: Tips, Templates, and Tools

This section will provide tips on how to create an end-of-the-semester reflection, which will elicit different aspects of students' learning and provide to you invaluable feedback. This reflection forces them to become mindful of the past semester and raise self-awareness. Learning to reflect is a skill that needs to be developed, and this is a way for them to look at how things went for them and what they could do differently to be more successful.

Tips

Course Reflection Questions

A powerful way to end a course is to provide students an opportunity to reflect on the knowledge they gained, the skills they developed, and the learning process(es) they have experienced. So often students are focused on their grades for the class instead of taking time to pause and reflect on what stood out most to them in their learning and how this class was relevant to their lives.

In a course reflection, students can be asked to write short statements in response to questions about the class. Here are several questions you can choose from, but there could be questions you want to ask if you do something different or new in your class and want their feedback:

- What was the most significant thing you learned in this class? Why?
- What did you expect to learn from this class? How did this course meet your expectations?
- What is one way you intend to use or apply your learning in this class in the future?
- What have you learned about yourself by taking this class remotely/online this term?
- Which activities or assignments helped you learn most? Why?
- What worked or did not work in helping you learn? (This could include something specific you do in class like exit tickets, etc., as an example.)
- If you could change anything about this course, what would it be?
- If you were to tell a future student what you liked about this class, what would you say?
- Get their opinion . . . What question(s) would you add to this list?

Tools

A valuable tool to use during a synchronous class is to change your virtual background for each class. A virtual background allows you to display an image as your background instead of what is naturally behind you. You can change your virtual background to the topic your students are going to be discussing during that particular class, or a theme, or something that is going on in the world or campus. It gives you the opportunity to have some fun and help depressurize things for students since they are probably very stressed out with class. The possibilities are endless!

Virtual Backgrounds

The virtual background sets the tone for your class and creates a warm and productive environment for the students to feel safe and comfortable. It also establishes a sense of professionalism because it shows that you are prepared to teach, and you have put time and effort into providing a friendly learning environment for all your students. Although virtual classrooms cannot mimic your in-person classroom, you can use a program like Canva to create some interesting backgrounds that can be fun and realistic. This is your chance to be creative, and it can be as simple or extravagant as you would like!

Some suggestions on virtual classroom backgrounds that students love to see are a world map, a picture of your actual physical classroom, a place to provide reminders (e.g., save the date, etc.), holiday celebrations, the U.S.

flag, your institution's logo, and so on. You could also change your background to align with your class session. It provides an interesting visual aid for the students during their time in a synchronous class session.

A website that provides different types of backgrounds is Capitalize My Title (capitalizemytitle.com). We provide a QR code to scan to access this website in Figure 2.9. This website provides personalized and fun virtual backgrounds for teachers, which are editable using Canva (an example of one is in Figure 2.10). Canva provides an easy drag-and-drop editing platform

Figure 2.9. Scan QR code to access Capitalize My Title website.

Figure 2.10. An example of a virtual background.

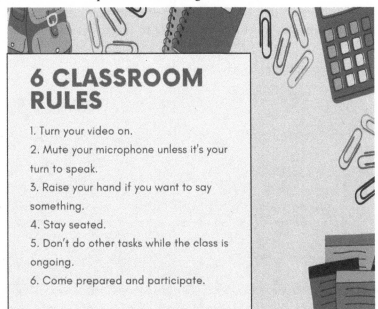

that lets you create your own color scheme and swap out fonts. You can also share this template with various social media and file-sharing sites or through email.

A simple Google search of Zoom virtual backgrounds will provide you with endless possibilities! Be creative and use the virtual backgrounds as a way for students to be engaged and excited to see what you put up next. If you get really good at changing them, you could even change them during your session! This is always fun when students come back from a short break and see a new background.

With this background, we took a screenshot of just the hanging sign that says, "Dr. Ricevuto will be right in," and we use that as a profile picture when the camera is off, instead of displaying an empty box with our name in it or our picture (Figure 2.11). We always have others on a virtual call complimenting the profile picture and wanting to know where we created it.

GREAT IDEA!

SlidesMania offers many templates for presentations and virtual backgrounds!

Another great tool to use is Slides Mania (https://slidesmania .com). (Use the Figure 2.12 QR code to access Slides Mania.) This tool can be used to change your background using one of the slides or used to create a PowerPoint presentation or Google slide presentation. We often use it to change the background that students will see on Zoom. We will change it to reflect a theme we are learning about or a season that is coming up. Everything on Slides Mania is free, and they also send you an email when they add new templates.

Figure 2.11. Example profile picture when camera is off.

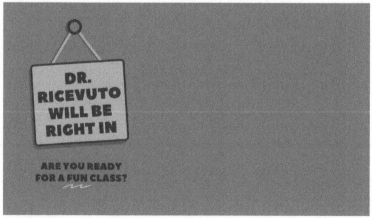

Figure 2.12. Scan QR code to access Slides Mania.

Figure 2.13 provides an example of a background used to reflect a season from Slidesmania.com. All these slides are provided for you to download and so that you may create a background with your own information.

Additionally, if you just want your background blurred, be sure to go into your Zoom virtual background setting and click on the blur background (Figure 2.14). We often use this function when we do not have

Figure 2.13. Example of a Slides Mania template reflecting the fall season.

Figure 2.14. Example of a Zoom blurred background.

time to create a background for our class, or do not want anyone seeing our setting. Zoom is constantly updating their platform, so be sure to get the updates by going to https://tinyurl.com/VISF-updates or scanning the QR code in Figure 2.15.

However, students *do* like seeing you in your natural settings too! For instance, during the semester I was in Mexico and taught my class from a resort with the ocean in the background and you could hear the waves (Figure 2.16). The students were all full of smiles for that class and were

Figure 2.15. Get updates for Zoom when available so you have the latest features.

Figure 2.16. Allow students to see you in natural settings.

actively asking me to show them the beach or the ocean or anything else because it was winter at home! Again, this just helps with the connections that you make with your students.

Wheel of Names

Interaction in a virtual environment is far more difficult than in a face-to-face classroom. As the instructor, you must be more deliberate about your student–student and student–teacher interactions. Depending on whether your class is asynchronous or synchronous, you can make use of discussion boards, group projects, chat boxes, and virtual programs like Jamboard and Padlet.

To be sure that every student in your class is participating, you can make use of a name generator like Wheel of Names (wheelofnames.com; Figure 2.17). Scan the QR code in Figure 2.18 to access the site. You can share your screen and show the wheel with everyone's name on it. Then virtually spin the wheel and a name is generated, and then it would be that student's turn to participate.

Jamboard

Using Jamboard, which is a cloud-based Google app, is an easy way to check in with your students. Jamboard is an online interactive whiteboard

Figure 2.17. Wheel of Names name generator to increase participation and build community in your virtual classroom.

Figure 2.18. Scan the QR code to access Wheel of Names.

(that looks like slides), which enables visual collaboration between users in real time. Jamboard as an app and a free platform that can be used on tablets, smartphones, and computers.

There are many free templates available on the internet; we suggest doing an internet search about Jamboard check-ins and see how many are listed. Then you can easily copy a template and use it for your own class. A website we use often is Ditch that Textbook (https://ditchthattextbook

Figure 2.19. Scan QR code to access Jamboard templates you can use.

.com/jamboard-templates/) which provides many free resources for teachers. This link will provide free Jamboard templates, which we have used many times or copied them and modified them to our liking (scan the QR code in Figure 2.19).

We will often create a blank Jamboard with a simple question asking how they are doing, and then they need to post a meme or "sticky note" describing how they feel. It does not take long to do a check-in at the beginning of every class; it might take 5 minutes, and then we try to review everyone's answer if we can.

We will discuss Jamboard frequently throughout the book, especially in chapter 4 when we discuss engagement in a synchronous class session. More information about using Jamboard for engagement purposes will follow in chapter 4.

Mentimeter

As mentioned earlier, Mentimeter is an interactive easy-to-use presentation tool that allows teachers to engage their students in real time with questions, polls, quizzes, word clouds, images, gifs, and more. When using Mentimeter, you can create fun and interactive presentations. It gives the audience a chance to interact with you by making use of all its features. Students do not have to download anything or create an account; Mentimeter is accessed by students entering in a code that you are provided with.

One of the features Mentimeter provides is creating a screen that shows a question or poll to the audience. Then the audience just enters the code seen on the screen and then is prompted to answer the question or poll. Additionally, when the instructor creates the questions or polls in the app, their answers can be displayed as a word cloud once all responses

Figure 2.20. Scan QR code to access Mentimeter.

are tallied. This all done in real time and the audience will see the questions and results as they are submitted. Scan the QR code in Figure 2.20 to access Mentimeter.

Using the Annotation Feature (or Something Similar) in Zoom
As the host in Zoom, we would share our screen in presentation mode for the students to see, or you could screenshot it as an image and share your screen with the picture showing. Provided you are sharing your screen, the students can click on View Options and then Annotate, which will be located at the top of the screen.

You and the students will see these annotation tools in Figure 2.21.

Here are Zoom's instructions for each tool in the toolbar:

- *Mouse:* Deactivate annotation tools and switch to your mouse pointer. This button is blue if annotation tools are deactivated.
- *Select* (only available if you started the shared screen or whiteboard): Select, move, or resize your annotations. To select several annotations at once, click and drag your mouse to display a selection area.
- *Text:* Insert text.
- *Draw:* Insert lines, arrows, and shapes.
- *Stamp:* Insert predefined icons like a checkmark or star.
- *Spotlight/Arrow/Vanishing Pen:* Turn your cursor into a spotlight or arrow.

Figure 2.21. Annotation tools available in Zoom.

- *Spotlight* (only available if you started the shared screen or whiteboard): Displays your mouse pointer to all participants when your mouse is within the area being shared. Use this to point out parts of the screen to other participants.
- *Arrow:* Displays a small arrow instead of your mouse pointer. Click to insert an arrow that displays your name. Each subsequent click will remove the previous arrow placed. You can use this feature to point out your annotations to other participants.
- *Eraser:* Click and drag to erase parts of your annotation.
- *Format:* Change the formatting options of annotations tools like color, line width, and font.
- *Undo:* Undo your latest annotation.
- *Redo:* Redo the latest annotation that you undid.
- *Clear:* Delete all annotations.
- *Save:* Save shared screen/whiteboard and annotations as a PNG or PDF. The files are saved to the local recording location.

An example of what the screen would look like in real time as students were annotating is provided in Figure 2.22.

Templates

A template is provided to you for Thank a Classmate, which is form where students take the time to thank their classmate(s) who have helped them during the semester. The template will suggest a format that students would be able to acknowledge their classmates.

Figure 2.22. Example of the screen while students are annotating.

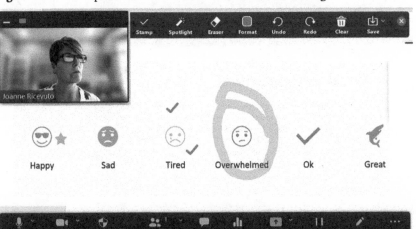

Thank a Classmate

Figure 2.23 provides an example of the Thank a Classmate program created in Google Forms.

Items on the form could include the following:

- Please add your first and last name. (If it is a relatively small class, you could have all students' names in a drop-down list that they would select from.)
- Please add your classmate's first and last name. (If it is a relatively small class, you could have all students' names in a drop-down list that they would select from.)
- How did your classmate help you understand concepts, feel comfortable in class, or complete assignments? Please be very thorough in explaining how they helped you.
- If I were to award extra credit points, how many points do you think they should receive and why?

In chapter 4, we will discuss how Google Forms can be used for a tool to get feedback from students on various items, and then in chapter 6, we will discuss how the tool can be used for assessment purposes.

Figure 2.23. Example of Thank a Classmate form.

Thank a Classmate

Please use this form to recognize your classmates' unseen work in this course with 1-2 extra credit points. If your classmates have helped you understand concepts, feel comfortable in class, or complete assignments, please indicate how they helped you, and suggest how many points you think this action deserves. Actions that can be recognized include, but are not limited to: offering feedback on your work, sharing notes, posing good questions, making helpful jokes, offering emotional support, or otherwise helping out

* Required

Wrapping It Up

In this chapter, you were provided with many tools and ideas to help you build community in your virtual classroom, including both you and the class. We wrap this section up with the following key points:

- Your role as a community builder and supporter begins with creating an atmosphere that students will feel comfortable in. You will want to create this environment by using many of the ideas laid out in this chapter; however, you do not have to use *all* of them.
- Many of the tools offered in this chapter will have to be prepared ahead of time. Remember, there are many tools available to choose from; focus on the tools that will help our students learn the best.
- Technology offers many powerful capabilities, and you now have many options. And remember, you do not have to use them *all*. Just take baby steps in the beginning until you are comfortable with teaching in the virtual classroom. Add things gradually, but as stated in the introduction, practice, practice, practice!
- Be as transparent as possible with your class and admit that you are not an expert, but you will be trying new things with them and that you want their feedback. They will respect you for saying this and admitting that you do not know everything there is to know about virtual teaching.

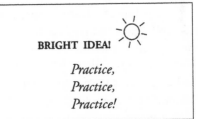

BRIGHT IDEA!

Practice,
Practice,
Practice!

In the next chapter, we will focus on team building in the virtual space. You will notice that as this chapter focused on community building with our students, faculty need to have the same opportunities with their colleagues. In this upcoming chapter, we share a multitude of ways to create these opportunities by using many different tools.

Chapter 2 Reflection Questions

1. How do you build community in your virtual classroom?
2. What tools do you use or plan to use to do this?
3. How do you personalize your course? Why is this important to you?
4. How can we continue to find creative ways to engage our learners?

VIRTUAL INSTRUCTOR AS A TEAM BUILDER, LEARNER, AND COLLABORATOR

The challenge these days is to be somewhere, to belong to some particular place, invest oneself in it, draw strength and courage from it, to dwell in community.

—bell hooks

In this chapter, we discuss the role of the virtual instructor as a team builder, learner, and collaborator—someone who connects with colleagues and peers to find ways to learn together and grow. The virtual instructor in the role of a team builder, learner, and collaborator not only connects with others but finds ways to help learners connect with each other in teams where they learn and collaborate. These teams can be formed through group projects that are developed and assigned to learners or informally where learners have opportunities within their virtual environment to interact and work with others. Within these team environments, virtual instructors have opportunities to build teaching presence as well as social and cognitive presence.

Part 1: Virtual Instructor as Team Builder, Learner, and Collaborator

Teaching in a virtual environment can be isolating and being part of learning communities can help create teaching presence as well as lessen this isolation. Jones (2011) conducted research during her virtual courses at the undergraduate and graduate level and concluded, "The instructor, as course designer and as facilitator, created a learning environment where students knew the course learning objectives, understood and followed the instructions, believed that the objectives were met, and believed they were part of a learning community created by the instructor and with other students" (p. 99). This creation of a learning community is something we will discuss within this chapter as an integral part of the role of the virtual instructor. Golden (2016) found that learning communities provided faculty with informal opportunities to share ideas and support each other, and this collaboration helped fuel innovation and creativity in the virtual environment. We believe it is not only important for instructors to create this environment within their virtual classes to build teaching presence and increase learning for their students, but also that instructors need to be part of a community of learners too.

Finding Your Team/Learning Community

We encourage everyone to find a team that you can call your own. Some of you may already have this team, and some of you may be actively seeking to work with others to share ideas and encourage each other. We have both been working with faculty in higher education for a long time, and we know the importance of collaborating with others in this work. Within our research, faculty were seeking opportunities to learn more from their colleagues, but they felt that time was not allotted for them to do this. They sought professional development (PD) opportunities to learn more, but they also wanted to attend PD that was meaningful and that provided information they could implement right away. Sometimes our best form of PD is right in front of us among our colleagues, but we need to find the time and space to make these connections and create this community of learning.

Virtual learning provides the flexibility to do this while balancing many other responsibilities, but sometimes you may need a reminder to see the team in your life or sometimes you may find that you need a new team. Coyle (2018) described three characteristics of a highly effective team, which are highlighted in Figure 3.1.

We have found these three characteristics to be critical when thinking about the qualities we want in our own learning communities.

FACULTY PERSPECTIVES

When asked what support they wished they had, faculty members responded:
"workshops and opportunities to collaborate with and learn from colleagues"

"more wellness check-ins for mental health and support"

Figure 3.1. Three characteristics that Coyle (2018) noted are important to look for in your team.

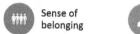 Sense of belonging

 Sharing of vulnerabilities

 Shared purpose/vision

Within higher education, a culture of competition sometimes causes work conflicts or a feeling of isolation (Olenick et al., 2019). This feeling of isolation can be magnified when working virtually, so we recommend intentionally finding opportunities to connect, collaborate, and work with others. Sometimes you may need to find others to work with outside of your department, school, or institution. That team, as some may call it, is a *community of practice*. And although this term has been around for a long time, implementing a community of practice within a virtual environment is relatively new. Golden (2016) conducted research on communities of practice implemented to support faculty who were primarily teaching virtually, and the themes identified within this research mimic Coyle's three points. Golden (2016) described the importance of shared practice and shared resources, building trust and creating a safe environment along with community building to prevent isolation, and opportunities for reflection and peer support.

We believe the first step toward creating this high-quality support team is to do the following: (a) identify your team and your shared interests, (b) find people who you can be open-minded with and who are willing to take risks and try something new, and (c) create an environment or join an environment where there is collaboration and shared tools, techniques, and research (Figure 3.2). Your support team may be where you currently work or maybe your team is someone you used to work with and are now in different institutions (e.g., the two authors). You may find that you have multiple support teams. The more the better.

 FACULTY PERSPECTIVES

Faculty member responses when asked what positives came out of teaching virtually in 2020:

"Students can review recorded material; students can collaborate in small groups, which they cannot do with the restrictions in place for social distancing in a classroom."

"It is a phenomenal opportunity to test new tools and expand the way we invite students into the learning journey."

"communicating with other teachers and talking about our struggles and successes together"

Figure 3.2. Identify-find-create—first steps toward a high-quality support team.

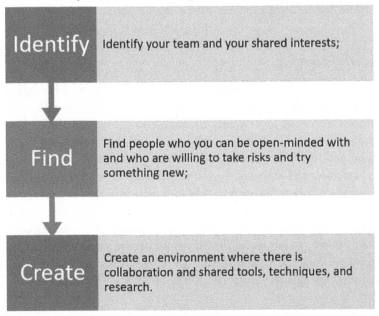

Figure 3.3. Framework for creating a high-quality virtual support team.

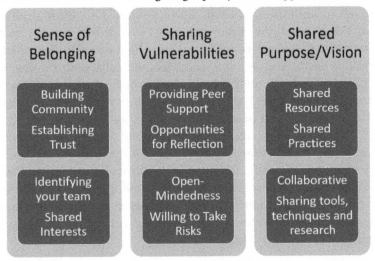

Figure 3.3 combines the ideas of Coyle (2018), Golden (2016), and our own ideas into a method we believe captures the framework for creating a high-quality, virtual instruction support team. We want our team to possess open-mindedness, a growth mindset, research-based ideas, and sharing

of tools and techniques freely, but this will only happen if we invest in the framework for creating a high-quality, virtual team.

Sense of Belonging

In chapter 2, we discussed many ways to create a sense of belonging and community within our virtual environments and in our virtual classrooms, but faculty also need to have this same sense of belonging within their own institutions and teams. When teams possess a sense of belonging, we believe the team will thrive and can help support each other in trying new things in virtual teaching and learning. To create this sense of belonging and community, it is important to be open to peer support and to also support peers. We want to model the same skills we expect our students to possess within their virtual environments. We can do this by finding our team, naming our team, and contributing to our team. Sometimes we have to take a risk and reach out to people we may not have worked with before. If you have shared interests in creating high-quality virtual environments, this is a great place to start.

Sharing of Vulnerabilities

To be able to work effectively with others, we should be able to share struggles as well as strengths within our team. Virtual learning can be challenging especially when we are trying something new. Finding colleagues with whom we can connect and share ideas and collaborate on what to do next can help. This can only happen when we open ourselves up to being honest and open-minded and when we have developed trust. Trust is a key factor that needs to be in place before sharing vulnerabilities. Golden (2016) shared the importance of communities of practice being "open and present in discussions concerning problems of practice and areas of insecurity or anxiety" (p. 88). We can establish trust by supporting our colleagues, celebrating their accomplishments, and helping to contribute to their growth and development. Also, a willingness to take a risk is part of being able to share vulnerabilities and working with colleagues who can try new tools or techniques together.

Shared Purpose and Vision

When we are part of a team where we have a shared purpose and vision, we can remind ourselves why we do what we do and supporting each other in these efforts is natural. Creating an environment where resources and ideas

Figure 3.4. Multiple suggestions for finding ways to collaborate virtually with other faculty.

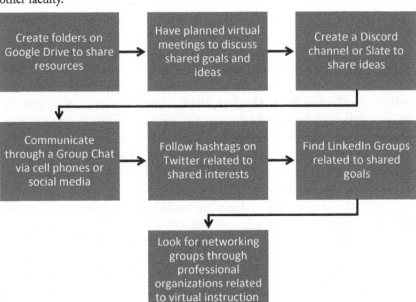

are freely shared can help to support our goals. Collaboration is something that can and should happen between faculty members. Further in this chapter, we will discuss ways to create shared spaces for our virtual classrooms, and these same ideas can be implemented between faculty members. The more we share with each other, the better we will all be when it comes to figuring out the virtual environment. Through our work with faculty members, we note the many ways they collaborate and find shared spaces, shared research, and shared ideas. Figure 3.4 highlights ideas on finding ways to collaborate with other faculty and share ideas. Connected educators freely share with others as well as look for opportunities to learn from others too (Whitaker et al., 2015).

Creating Virtual Teams in Virtual Classrooms

To create a community of inquiry in the virtual classroom, one important component is to create virtual teams. Collaborative group work provides opportunities for students to interact virtually with each other, building community, and creating a greater sense of belonging within a virtual environment (Johnson et al., 2018). The framework we created in Figure 3.3 can be used to ensure students have opportunities to be part of an energizing, highly effective team—the same highly effective team we want to be part of as faculty members. Although collaborating virtually may seem challenging to some students, it is an excellent way to keep our students engaged and learning from each other. The cognitive presence we discussed in chapter 1 is built through these kinds of activities and practices where learners can engage with other learners. Combining a variety of strategies that engage students via learner to learner, learner to instructor, and learner to course content was found to be important in virtual instruction (Bolliger & Martin, 2018; Fletcher, 2020). When students have opportunities to work with others and discuss the course content, the projects they are completing, and the research they are conducting, their cognition and learning will most likely deepen. In addition, we all know one of the greatest ways to learn content is to teach others. So, we recommend having students present their ideas virtually to their classmates and to share resources with each other. For example, if you are teaching a course on diversity, you might have students join book study groups on different books you want the class to explore. Everyone will not be able to read all the books, but the groups will present their chosen book to the class virtually. This collaborative assignment shares the learning load and provides students with more content than they would have been able to cover on their own. Groups can record their presentation using a voice recording tool such as VoiceThread and then other students can answer or ask questions, so the presentation is interactive and collaborative.

In Table 3.1, we italicized the specific ways that virtual teams can create presence in a virtual environment. When an instructor creates opportunities for collaboration and shared learning, this helps to build social, teaching, and cognitive presence. These three presences are the critical components to creating a community of inquiry. Although students may not be in a physical classroom with their peers, these opportunities for collaboration can help to build connections and result in deeper and richer learning.

Allowing Choice in Virtual Learning Communities

Keeping in mind that virtual learning should provide flexibility for students, allowing choice within virtual learning communities is helpful. Just like we might want to choose the faculty we collaborate with, students can benefit from having opportunities to choose their teams too. If students need assistance or prefer to be placed in a team by the instructor, this can be a choice too. We provide the following suggestions in Figure 3.5 regarding allowing choice within virtual teams. We mentioned creating a student-centered ecosystem in chapter 1, and allowing choice is aligned

TABLE 3.1
Examples of Social, Teaching, and Cognitive Presence

Social Presence	Teaching Presence	Cognitive Presence
Getting to know other students	Getting to know the teacher	*Making sense of the content*
Expressing emotions and opinions	One-on-one meetings/ conversations with the teacher	*Discussing the content for further understanding*
Creating opportunities for collaboration	Asking the teacher questions	*Digging deeper and taking part in project-based learning, service learning, research*
Sharing a story	Engaging with teacher-directed assignments	Having students respond to other students
Building classroom community; supporting each other	Introducing a topic or project	Sharing knowledge and work with each other
Check-ins	Planning and preparing online course for student engagement	Providing peer feedback
Creating a sense of belonging	*Creating an environment that is authentic and supportive*	Using multimodal modes of instruction—videos, readings, resources

Figure 3.5. Suggestions on allowing choice within virtual teams to not only help engage students but also provide the flexibility that is valued in engaging virtual teaching and learning.

Choose their team   Choose the topic   Choose the timeline and due date   Choose the method they will share their work   Choose the tool they will use to present and collaborate

with this theory. Virtual instruction can provide flexibility that increases access, removes barriers, and helps students succeed (Boston Consulting Group, 2018). When students can set their own timelines and choose the tool, the group they will work with, and the project they will focus on, all of these choices can increase flexibility and options for students who may have been challenged otherwise.

If students/groups need help in deciding what tool to choose for a project or how to demonstrate their learning, you can provide them with a choice board where they can decide on what tool to use and methods to demonstrate learning. Table 3.2 provides an example of a tic-tac-toe choice board provided to students and is based on varying levels of Bloom's

TABLE 3.2

Example of a Tic-Tac-Toe Choice Board Used to Encourage Learners to Choose How They Will Demonstrate Their Learning as Well as Suggestions for Tools They Can Use

Tic-Tac-Toe Menu

A suggested tool is noted in each cell as well as what level of Bloom's Taxonomy would be addressed within each cell. Once you make a copy, you can change any of this to make it work for you and your students!

Collect	Teach	Interview
Facts or ideas which are important to you and create a digital bulletin board. (Padlet) (Knowledge)	Record yourself teaching the course content and share this recording with your classmates. (Flipgrid) (Synthesis)	Two different people about an issue. Share the results of the interview and your takeaways in a presentation (Google Slides) (Evaluation)
Create		**Graph**
An original game using the facts you have learned and share with the class. (Kahoot) (Synthesis)	**Free Space**	Some part of your study to show what you learned and what others should know about the topic - include an explanation of the data. (Desmos) (Analysis)
Write	**Survey**	**Demonstrate**
A blog on the content area you are exploring and publish it! (WordPress) (Evaluation)	Others to learn their opinions about some fact, idea, or feature of your study and then analyze the results and share with the class. (Google Forms) (Analysis)	What you have learned and share this demonstration in a video. (YouTube) (Application)

Figure 3.6. Scan this QR code to access a tic-tac-toe choice template you can modify and use if desired. We use choice often and provide a tic-tac-toe board where learners can choose options, allowing flexibility and creativity.

taxonomy. This choice board can be modified and used for any course topic and with a variety of technology tools. We provide a QR code in Figure 3.6 that you can scan and access. The free space allows the students to choose a technology we may not be aware of or that is not listed. One thing we have learned is that we can learn about tools and technologies from the students we teach too.

Sharing Work With Other Teams

Providing teams with project ideas that are meaningful and tied to real life situations will increase student engagement and motivation and help support a learning community. Cooperative assignments are considered high-impact projects and research suggests that these practices increase student engagement and learning (Kuh & O'Donnell, 2013). Further, Kuh and O'Donnell (2013) identified multiple characteristics of high-impact practices (Figure 3.7). We will talk more about authentic assessments in chapter 6, but we know how collaborative team projects can create a shared learning community for students. We suggest using a shared space like Google Drive and creating shared folders and/or shared documents where teams can see, interact, and comment on other teams' work. The benefit of using a shared space (other than the course LMS) is that when the course is over, the learning can still take place and learners still have access to course materials and resources. If everything was only shared within the course LMS, this collaboration and access ends when the course ends.

Figure 3.7. Framework to consider when creating high-impact practices in our virtual environments where a learning community can thrive (Kuh & O'Donnell, 2013).

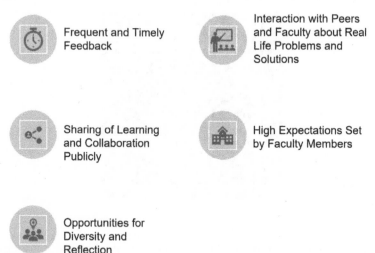

Frequent and Timely Feedback

Interaction with Peers and Faculty about Real Life Problems and Solutions

Sharing of Learning and Collaboration Publicly

High Expectations Set by Faculty Members

Opportunities for Diversity and Reflection

Within one shared Google document, students can sign up for their project either individually or in groups, and then provide a link to their project with the class on this same page when they have completed it. Then the students can peer review and comment on the other teams' or students' work. An example of this is provided in Table 3.3 where students were asked to choose which book they wanted to read and present on and then they would work with their team to create a VoiceThread presentation that was interactive where other groups would respond. This allowed the students to gain more knowledge about the content without having to read all three books. The students were also able to share responsibility within their project and focus on specific areas. This kind of collaborative virtual group work creates cognitive and social presence and ensures that learners are actively engaged. Students were able to read a book they chose and present it in an engaging way with their classmates.

Stressing Individual Accountability

Although we hope that all team collaboration is positive and that all students are accountable, sometimes this may not be the case. Ouyang and Chang (2019) suggested "assigning students with leadership roles (e.g., learning

TABLE 3.3
Example of Book Study Collaborative Project

Book Study and Presentation on Topic Related to Culturally Responsive Teaching

Please choose one of the books below and sign up for what book you choose, plan to obtain this book either at the local library or on Amazon, set a timeline for reading this book (the course is accelerated, so you can start beforehand), set a time to meet with your group to discuss the book by week 3 of our course, and then plan a collaborative presentation with your group that you will upload and voice or audio record in VoiceThread so your classmates can interact and answer questions in VoiceThread by week 8.

Your presentation should be informative: include tips and suggestions teachers can do related to the book topic, ask reflective questions and engage classmates in discussions on VoiceThread, and provide a resource that can be shared to other teachers and administrators: Book Study and Presentation Sign Up.

Becoming a White Anti-Racist: A Practical Guide for Educators, Leaders, and Activists **by Brookfield & Hess (2021)**

Your name	Links to Presentation and Resources

Antiracism and Universal Design for Learning: Building Expressways to Success **by Andratesha Fritzgerald (2020). (Foreword by Samaria Rice, mother of Tamir Rice)**

Your name	Links to Presentation and Resources

Culturally Responsive Teaching and the Brain **by Zaretta Hammond (2015)**

Your name	Links to Presentation and Resources

designers and facilitators) could empower inactive students to move from peripheral participation to active participation" (p. 1408). Additionally, students who are connected to their classmates and classroom community (chapter 2) are more likely to engage in class discussions and assignments. Group collaboration can certainly help increase cognitive presence in the course as we discussed in this chapter, but it may also hinder students if the appropriate supports are not in place. Stressing to our students that online collaboration is important, but that also we understand their need for flexibility, can help create that balance and awareness in the groups that they too should be flexible and understanding.

If someone has work and life obligations that deter them from joining a live session for their group collaboration, the group should be encouraged to come up with alternative ways the group members can contribute asynchronously. If learning is shared and students are learning and collaborating, how and when they do it should not be dictated to them. However, if students are encountering challenges within their group collaboration, they should be encouraged to seek assistance from the instructor, after trying to work it out with the group, for advice and direction. One suggestion would be to have a rubric that grades students both individually for some parts of the assignment and as a group for other parts of the assignment. Students should know that if either they or a group member is not contributing, they will not receive credit for the work others in their group did. The Quality Matters (2020) rubric standard 3.3 states "specific and descriptive criteria are provided for the evaluation of learners' work, and their connection to the course grading policy is clearly explained." This is especially important when requiring our students to work in groups and how they are being measured should be evident to them and their group members prior to beginning the group project or assessment.

Class Discussion and Engagement

Asynchronous class discussions are a popular and frequent strategy used to increase cognitive presence and encourage collaboration within a virtual environment (Ouyang & Chang, 2019). Aderibigbe (2020) stated "students indicated that they find colleagues' feedback, response, and efforts helpful, along with the instructor's feedback, and clear guidelines are useful and motivating in the online discussions" (p. 12). The Student Engagement component of the Quality Course Teaching and Instructional Practice scorecard (OLC, 2016) provides guidance to virtual instructors on class discussions and engagement. The categories in this section of the scorecard can help you assess your online discussions and prepare for discussions that prompt student-to-student and student-to-instructor interaction as well as student-to-content engagement. The following connects the points within the scorecard on classroom discussion and engagement and their relation to cognitive, social, and teaching presence:

- The instructor creates meaningful discussions aligned to course learning outcomes and provides opportunities for critical thinking (teaching and cognitive presence).
- The instructor is present within the discussions by responding, highlighting, and facilitating throughout the discussion (teaching presence).
- Questions posed are reflective and thought-provoking (cognitive presence).
- Learners are provided with a clear description of what is expected of them for participation in the class discussion (teaching presence) and the purpose of the discussion and responding to classmates is part of this participation (social presence).
- Diverse perspectives are valued, and students are asked to be aware of diverse perspectives and respectful of others (social presence).

Virtual instructors can "create a safe, collaborative, and enabling online discussion forum where students can freely participate and provide feedback" (Aderibigbe, 2020, p. 12). Using the course LMS discussion board is one way to engage students in these discussions, but we also use other tools such as Flipgrid, Padlet, VoiceThread, and Socrative to ask learners to engage with one another, answer reflective questions, and pose their own questions. We know the importance of engaging frequently within these discussions, but also letting our students and learners engage and share their own thinking and learning. Learners should be encouraged to move the discussion forward by asking thought-provoking questions, sharing resources, and answering questions that others posed to them. Learners can also visit the discussions multiple times during the time that the discussion is open so they can engage with the content, with the instructor, and with each other. We know it can be difficult to respond to every comment a student makes, but we have found it helpful to provide a summary with highlighted comments at the end of the discussion. The summary with highlighted comments can be sent via the LMS Announcements as a wrap-up at the end of a module.

THE BOTTOM LINE

Create engaging, thought-provoking discussions that learners want to revisit and engage in conversation around.

An example of a rubric that can be used to evaluate discussion boards or VoiceThread responses can be found in Table 3.4. The more clarity you provide your students related to how they will be assessed, the better their experience and learning will be. The Quality Matters (2020) rubric suggests including the following when it comes to discussion board assessments:

- clear description of how learners' participation will be graded with the number of posts expected and criteria for evaluating the depth and quality of the posting
- expectations for posting to classmates and how these posts are evaluated

Evaluating the Tool

In chapter 1, we introduced an evaluation tool that we use when considering integration into our teaching for a specific purpose. We stress the importance of not using a tool just to use a tool, but to decide first if this is a tool that will work for the purpose you are targeting. There are many tools that can help with collaboration and increasing cognition in a course. Because we mentioned VoiceThread as an example within this chapter, we will use the Evaluating the Tool form to demonstrate how to go through this step of the process. Not only are we considering the tool, but we are considering the assessment and how our students could best demonstrate their learning virtually. In Table 3.5, we determine that VoiceThread for the purpose of this group assignment would be used to build cognitive presence where students will dig deeper and share their learning with each other through this tool. Although this tool may not be embedded into the course LMS, it is a tool that can be embedded into the LMS. However, students can use the free version of VoiceThread by having one student take on the responsibility of uploading the content they want in the presentation, and then sharing the VoiceThread so the other team members can comment on the slides to add their thoughts. The instructor can also add their thoughts to increase teaching presence and then students in other groups can also listen and respond to join in on the learning. Because VoiceThread provides options such as using your voice, text, or video to respond, this can provide accessibility and versatility to both the learners and instructors.

TABLE 3.4

Rubric: Discussion Board/VoiceThread Posts

CATEGORY	5	4	3	1
Critical Thinking (5 pts)	Conveys significant depth of thought through reflection and new ideas supported by outside readings/resources (incorporates relevant multimedia)	Demonstrates some depth of thought and may include new ideas and/or supporting references	Very little original thought, mostly summarizes or restates information from assigned reading	No evidence of critical thinking, synthesis, or reflection
Collaboration/ Contribution (10 pts)	Participates actively by responding to other posts and contributing meaningful questions and/or comments that prompt further discussion	Responds to other posts but may not serve to promote further discussion	Mostly superficial posts with little engagement in overall discussion	Does not respond to other posts or interact within the discussion thread
Promptness/ Deadlines (5 pts)	Post(s) submitted on time and early enough to engage further discussion	Post(s) submitted 1–2 days late	Post(s) submitted 3–4 days late	Post(s) submitted 5+ days late
Organization (5 pts)	Well-organized; logical sequence of ideas	Mostly organized and logical	Little evidence of structure	Poorly written; disorganized
References and Support (10 pts)	Uses references that go beyond personal experience or course material in ways that strongly support the main position	Appeals to the work/ arguments of other students, scholars, and experts; references source material correctly and precisely	Appeals only to personal experience as support or only references source material in general ways	No or few references or support for position

TABLE 3.5
Evaluating the Tool—VoiceThread Example

Name of Tool	Building Social Presence (list how)	Building Teaching Presence (list how)	Building Cognitive Presence (list how)	Tool is embedded in the LMS or has capability to be embedded into the LMS (Yes or No)	Format: Asynchronous Synchronous Face-to-Face Dual Learner
VoiceThread: https://voicethread.com/myvoice/		Instructors can share their responses on the VoiceThread and help affirm student responses, add information, and clarify misconceptions.	For this assignment, students will present their book study presentation providing content to their peers with interactive questions to engage them.	VT can be embedded into the LMS, but it is not embedded into the LMS at my institution.	Asynchronous collaboration with team members; asynchronous feedback from instructor
Comments	I like giving my students a chance to hear each other talk within a VoiceThread discussion. I think that students can also learn a lot from using this tool to present and talk about what they are learning—this goes back to building cognitive presence by having students make sense of their learning. The peer comments can also help my students learn from each other and build off each other's ideas. The instructor's comments can help increase teacher presence as well as cognitive presence too.				

Name of Tool	Building Social Presence (list how)	Building Teaching Presence (list how)	Building Cognitive Presence (list how)	Tool is embedded in the LMS or has capability to be embedded into the LMS (Yes or No)	Format: Asynchronous Synchronous Face-to-Face Dual Learner
Questions to Consider					
What organizational resources do you need to implement this tool?			Discuss with the institution to see whether VoiceThread can be embedded into the LMS. If not, is there funding available to purchase the instructor version of VoiceThread? There is a free version, but it limits my ability to make just five threads in total.		
What support do you need to use the tool besides an internet connection?			I would like to discuss with other faculty who also use this tool to see what tips they may have for me or suggestions in using the tool to its fullest capacity.		
What is your backup plan if the tool does not work or does not accomplish what you thought it would?			I would first want to figure out what did not work and why it did not work. If students are not able to comment on the VoiceThread, I would first ask them to use a different browser and a different device. If it still does not work, I would have an alternative way for them to respond, such as in a traditional discussion board.		

Part 2: Tips, Tools, and Templates to Support the Virtual Instructor as a Team Builder, Learner, and Collaborator

In this section, we provide resources to support the virtual instructor as a team builder, learner, and collaborator and one who develops and is part of communities of practice.

Tips

We provide the following tips related to using rubrics to assess group work and using tools to create and make rubrics. We include tips related to checking in and providing incremental due dates, if appropriate.

Creating Rubrics for Virtual Group Work

Table 3.6 provides a rubric where students are being assessed on both individual and group parts of this assignment. This rubric can be modified and used for different assignments and a QR code is provided within the Template section of this chapter for your use. There are many websites that provide support for creating free rubrics. We have found the following websites to be helpful when creating rubrics:

- Rubistar: http://rubistar.4teachers.org/index.php
- Rubric Maker: https://rubric-maker.com/
- Quick Rubric: https://www.quickrubric.com/
- Cornell's Center for Teaching Innovation has a good sample of a group rubric: https://teaching.cornell.edu/resource/example-group-work-rubric

When creating rubrics for group assignments, we recommend the following:

- Break down the individual responsibilities as well as the group responsibilities of the assignment.
- Break the project up into smaller deliverables with varying due dates if possible.
- Include a reflection where students can share their personal experience and the experience they had working within their group.
- Include a peer review component where groups peer review other teams' projects.

Set Up Meetings With Teams

We also recommend setting up meetings with the teams individually to check in with how things are going, answer any questions, and build on

TABLE 3.6
Rubric: Group Coaching and Feedback Assignment

CATEGORY	4	3	2	1
Preparation (30 pts) Individual points	Submits something to the group that is connected to course topic and submits in a timely manner and demonstrates thought for what is submitted	Submits something to the group that is connected to course topic	Submits something to the group that is not closely connected to course topic	Submits nothing to the group
Collaboration (30 pts) Group points	Group interactions are shared in a way where everyone can see the communication; communication is collaborative, timely, professional, and reflective	Group interactions are shared in a way where everyone can see the communication	Group interactions are not shared where everyone can see the communication	Group interactions do not occur
Feedback provided—connection to course resources, text, etc. (30 pts) Individual points	Feedback provided shows in-depth understanding of topic, refers to specific ideas and suggestions	Feedback provided shows understanding of topic but lacks depth	Feedback provided is basic but does not show a clear understanding of topic	Shows little understanding of topic or is not connected to topic
Insights gathered (30 pts) Individual points	Three or four underlying concepts presented and connected to feedback given	Two underlying concepts presented and connected to feedback given	One underlying concept presented and connected to feedback given	No underlying concepts presented and no connections to feedback given
Creativity (30 pts) Group points	Interaction and ways this group coaching and feedback is presented demonstrates creativity and is meaningful and reflective of the course topic	Interaction and ways this group coaching and feedback is presented demonstrates creativity	Interaction and ways this group coaching and feedback is presented and shared with the group does not demonstrate creativity	Nothing is shared with the group

the cognitive presence within the teams. Teams can be encouraged to invite you to a team meeting so that you can answer the questions at a time that works for the students or if time constraints permit this from happening, teams can send questions via email. The goal is for the teams to be self-directed in completing their work but knowing that you are available to support and scaffold as needed is of great importance. If teams are having challenges collaborating, you can offer suggestions on how to accomplish the goal asynchronously. Some team members may have more availability than others, and it is important to remind the members of the need for flexibility and the diversity of responsibilities that others in their group may have.

Check-Ins or Incremental Due Dates

Asking teams to provide progress reports or updates periodically throughout the course is a good idea. During whole group synchronous sessions, groups can each share their updates verbally. Another option is to have the teams contribute to a Google form or a shared Google document, and then the updates can be shared with the whole group. These check-ins would also give teams an opportunity to gather ideas that are working for other teams that they may be able to use. The more interaction between the teams and sharing of knowledge and ideas, the stronger the virtual learning community will become. Something else we have tried is to have incremental due dates for a project. Instead of having the one final due date, have three separate due dates (these can also be set by the teams to be flexible), and the project is then broken up into three parts—part one, part two, and part three. The three parts together create the larger project, but teams will be able to obtain feedback, share their learning, and modify, if necessary, along the way.

Skills for a Lifetime

If learners are concerned about being assigned a virtual group project, remind them of the benefits of working together. Collaboration and communication with a diverse group of people are skills that are necessary and will last a lifetime. In work and life, we will always have to work with other people in some capacity, so why not help students gain these skills and appreciate learning these skills? As we all learned in 2020, virtual collaboration was possible and effective and sometimes is the only way we can communicate and collaborate. Remember that virtual learning can be isolating if learners do not have the chance to work with others. That group project may be the only time they can meet someone in their degree program. Stress to your students the benefits of having a team/learning community and how this collaboration can bring joy, diversity, and lifetime skills they will need.

Tools

We provide suggested tools for you to try when building a virtual learning community. There are so many tools to choose from, but we only provide a few that at the time of this publication were ones that we used and have found to be helpful and user-friendly. We challenge you to find a partner or a team, as we described in the beginning of this chapter, and try something new with them supporting you and collaborating with you along the way.

Trello

Trello is a digital project management tool that is visual, free, and can be used at an instructor level to organize a semester, a course, or a project. Trello can also be used at the team or group level for individual groups to use to organize their work. We created a Trello board to demonstrate how we could organize the writing of this book and keep track of our timeline, who was working on what chapter, and when each of our chapters was completed (see Figure 3.8).

Figure 3.8. Sample Trello board created to show collaboration on this book with the authors.

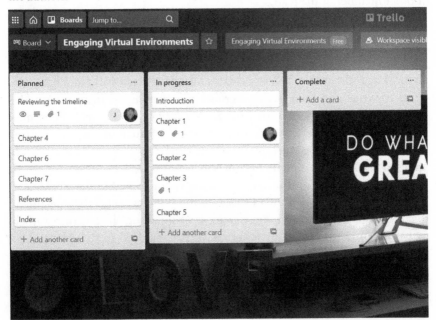

Trello is easy to use and can be set up in many ways. Some instructors use Trello to organize their syllabus and invite their students to their Trello board to contribute and add content to make the syllabus dynamic and student driven. The smallest unit of the Trello board is what they call cards. The cards are used to represent tasks and ideas. For each card that is created, members can be assigned various tasks to complete with due dates. So, for writing this book, we could each be assigned cards for the chapters we were focusing on. As we complete and update our chapters, we can make notes in our cards. These cards can be moved when the tasks are in progress or when they are completed. This also allows some flexibility as sometimes assignments need to be changed or due dates need to be extended. Individual students can keep track of these changes and post questions right in Trello to their instructor.

Groups can use the Trello app to organize a group project. New members can be invited to the board and assigned tasks at different times. Other teams can be invited to see the work that is in progress and to collaborate between teams on specific cards. Trello contributes to creating a cognitive presence in a virtual environment by having learners work together, organize their thoughts and ideas, and contribute to projects. Trello provides a visual to quickly see what tasks have been completed and which ones are still being worked on. Individual group members can be notified if they have missed a due date and other team members can see if they need to provide support to another member of the team.

Slack or Discord

Slack or Discord are discussion boards where you can have conversations about your course topic. You can create collaborative networks and have students converse and share across sections and even across institutions. The benefit of using these tools is that you can create an open channel of communication, and this also creates an archive of this information for use later on. You can create separate workspaces for each course you are teaching or each semester if you want students to converse between sections. After you create the separate workspace, you can then create channels within the workspace. For example, if we created a workspace for this book, we might have channels that look like this: #general, #resources, #collaboration. If someone wanted to have a conversation about resources, they would go to that channel to leave their message.

Wakelet

Think of Wakelet as a public, open version of Pinterest. We have used Wakelet to gather materials and have students post their resources within a shared online location. Wakelet is easy to use and free. The first step is to create a board and then invite others to contribute to the board. Groups can create their own boards and then share their boards with other groups. The students received credit for adding their resources and they also had the opportunity to learn about resources from their peers. Wakelet can also be used in a faculty learning community to gather and share resources with each other. These types of activities are collaborative and also help to create that shared purpose and ownership.

Templates

The templates we provide in this section can be copied, modified and used in your own virtual environments.

QR Code for Evaluating the Tool Template

We provide the following template for you to use to evaluate tools you are considering using in your virtual environment (Figure 3.10).

Figure 3.10. Use this QR code to scan and access the Evaluating the Tool template we use throughout the book to evaluate tools we are using. You can copy the document and use for your own evaluation of tools.

Figure 3.11. Scan this QR code to access the Group Coaching and Feedback Rubric—feel free to make a copy and modify for your own use.

QR Code for Rubric: Group Coaching and Feedback
You can scan the QR code in Figure 3.11 to access the Rubric for Group Coaching and Feedback to copy, modify, and use this template for your own use if applicable.

Wrapping It Up

In this chapter, we discussed the virtual instructor role of team builder, learner, and collaborator. We suggest the following:

- Find your own team or learning community—one where you can develop a strong sense of belonging, where you have opportunities to share vulnerabilities (especially when related to virtual teaching and learning), and where there is a shared vision and goals.
- Create opportunities for your students to be a part of a team or learning community where they can grow and develop as learners and where they have a shared purpose and shared ownership for learning.
- Support your students to be self-directed and accountable for their own learning by providing them with meaningful opportunities to learn from the course content, from you and from their classmates.

In the following chapter, we discuss the importance of creating engaging synchronous environments.

Chapter 3 Reflection Questions

1. What are some creative ways we can engage with other faculty members in exploring virtual teaching and learning?
2. Who are the team members we can call on to support us when we need support? If you do not have specific people identified, what steps will you take to create your team?
3. How can you support other faculty members? How can we support each other and provide encouragement as we struggle through the challenges presented through virtual teaching and learning?

VIRTUAL INSTRUCTOR AS A COURSE DESIGNER AND STUDENT ENGAGER

Using Synchronous Instruction

If we're growing, we're always going to be out of our comfort zones.

—John C. Maxwell

If we teach today's students as we taught yesterday's, we rob them of tomorrow.

—John Dewey

In this chapter we will define the roles of virtual instructor as a course designer and student engager and then focus on how to provide an engaging virtual space specifically in a synchronous session.

Part 1: Describing the Role of Virtual Instructor as a Course Designer and Student Engager in Synchronous Sessions

In chapter 2, we explained the benefits of creating a landing page and how to do check-ins with students, and this chapter will expand on ways to build community and create teaching presence in a synchronous setting. We will be using some of the same tools introduced in chapter 2 for check-ins, but here apply them to engaging students during synchronous sessions. Then throughout this chapter there will be many new tools that will be mentioned to create an engaging space, as well as how we can use gamification and platforms like Kahoot! to keep our students engaged.

Defining the Role of Virtual Instructor as a Course Designer and Student Engager

We define the *role of a virtual instructor as a course designer and student engager* as an instructor who will plan, design, and build an online course that will incorporate best practices where the student can be fully engaged.

As stated in chapter 1, we need to focus on purpose and what tool/ program/technology will help us build a specific presence. In this chapter we will be focusing on *teaching presence* and keeping these items in mind as well as other ways to build social, teaching, and cognitive presence (Table 4.1).

BRIGHT IDEA!

Create an engaging online space for students.

TABLE 4.1
Examples of Social, Teaching, and Cognitive Presence

Social Presence	*Teaching Presence*	*Cognitive Presence*
Getting to know other students	Getting to know the teacher	Making sense of the content
Expressing emotions and opinions	One-on-one meetings/ conversations with the teacher	Discussing the content for further understanding
Creating opportunities for collaboration	*Asking the teacher questions*	Digging deeper and taking part in project-based learning, service learning, research
Sharing a story	*Engaging with teacher-directed assignments*	Having students respond to other students
Building classroom community; supporting each other	*Introducing a topic or project*	Sharing knowledge and work with each other
Check-ins	*Planning and preparing online course for student engagement*	Providing peer feedback
Creating a sense of belonging	*Creating an environment that is authentic and supportive*	Using multimodal modes of instruction— videos, readings, resources

One of the many lessons we learned from supporting faculty during virtual teaching and learning was that faculty began to realize that they could not conduct their synchronous classes as they did when they were in the classroom. For that reason, this whole chapter will focus on the many ideas of how to keep students engaged during a synchronous session.

Virtual teaching is here to stay. Higher education has been transformed, and students will start to see technology integrated into their classes in intentional ways that will differentiate their experiences. To continue this transformation, teachers need to embrace technology to make learning more engaging. Technology needs to be used by both students *and* teachers, for this is the "paper and pencil" of our time, and both need to use it well. The integration of effective technology offers opportunities for students to be actively involved in the learning process. When students are fully engaged and they're interested in what they're doing in class, that is where the real learning takes place. However, teachers need to integrate technology into their curriculum and teaching instead of viewing it as an add-on, because technology is the lens through which we now experience our world. And you can't connect your students to the world if you aren't connected to it yourself!

Begin With Your LMS Tools

Regardless of which LMS your institution uses—Canvas, Blackboard, Schoology, Google Classroom, and so on, your LMS is vital in an online learning environment and should play a significant role in your course. It is tempting to build your course in your LMS and then put it aside; however, it should evolve and change as the semester unfolds.

Establish Clear Routines

It's important to establish clear routines and expectations early on in your course. You need to be consistent and continue your routines all throughout the semester. This will help students become organized and less anxious when they know the routines and expectations of the class. You need to constantly remind your students of the routines and expectations and making use of the LMS announcement tool is very beneficial. As stated in chapter 2, a simple good morning message to the students could be sent out before class begins that would remind students of what is expected for that upcoming class as well as assignments due.

BRIGHT IDEA!

Establish routines and expectations early on in your course.

Review LMS Fundamentals With Students

Students are often anxious about coming into an online class for many reasons; however, you can eliminate these feelings if you provide a review of the fundamentals of the LMS. You could offer a low-stakes assessment to help students navigate and learn the LMS fundamentals. Students could get acquainted with how to view an assignment, how to submit assignments, how to access feedback from the instructor, accessing course materials, and so forth. Provide time during class to ensure every student masters this foundational knowledge before the first assignment is due.

GREAT IDEA!

Use a getting-acquainted first assignment to help students navigate the LMS.

Use the Rubric Feature

Your LMS provides a rubric feature that you should take full advantage of. Don't wait until the end of an assignment or assessment to use this helpful feature. Instead, use the rubric feature to help you provide feedback to students easily through the LMS. Students will benefit when they are able to utilize your feedback to monitor and improve their work moving forward, so providing students with a rubric with the assignment will guide them on your expectations for that assessment.

Best Practices in Using Your LMS

Here is a list of best practices when creating your course in your LMS. These should be careful considerations when preparing for your online course, which can be adjusted as the semester progresses as needed:

- Be consistent in formatting your assignments. Take into consideration how you want students to submit their work and if there is a rubric created to go along with it.
- Chunk text by using numbered lists and bullet points for simplifying instructions.
- Consider which font size to use and its readability. Many students will read items on their cell phones.
- Avoid cognitive overload with too many images, links, videos, etc. Design each page thoughtfully: everything you add should have a purpose.
- Consider making use of a voice app or video to help explain an assignment. Some students appreciate hearing or watching a video

that would help them understand what the expectations are for an assignment.

- Be mindful of integrating other online tools. Just as you might be apprehensive about using different technology, so might the students. When integrating a new tool, be sure to review with the students how to use it before an assignment is due. Written instructions are beneficial as is providing a video and/or voice app to explain how to use it.

Getting in Sync: Tools to Engage Students During a Synchronous Session

One of the key factors in engagement is *relevance*; teachers need to make the content that students are learning relevant to their everyday lives. Integrating microactivities into your classes is one sure way for students to get engaged. These microactivities are activities that you do throughout the synchronous session that keep students involved and engaged the whole time. Examples of these microactivities are listed in the text that follows, which can include games and engaging activities in your synchronous session. Engaging students in the learning process increases learners' attention and focus, their motivation to want to learn, and it helps promote meaningful learning experiences and drives desired outcomes.

THE BOTTOM LINE

Make content that they are learning relevant to their everyday lives.

Polling

One of the ways to begin a synchronous class is to ask them to participate in a poll with questions that are content related that could be related to their past experiences. For example, in our classes we discuss working in early childhood and what kinds of experiences they have encountered, which will lead into many of our discussions for class. So, before the lecturing begins, a poll is launched to get their anonymous feedback on their experiences.

GREAT IDEA!

In polling, ask questions that are relevant to their past experiences!

Polling is a quick, engaging way to ask questions to your audience in real time, and then share the results after. Polls include a question and response option, which creates an interactive experience for your students. Polls generate engagement through active responses, which in turn will spark conversation through further discussion around the poll topics and responses. The more relevant the questions are to the learners, the more engaged the students will be in the learning.

Students enjoy giving their anonymous opinion on questions because it's low risk, but they also enjoy it because it demonstrates to them that their opinion is valuable. Asking students for their opinion signals that you care about what they have to say. In doing so, you will also drive their interest in the content that will be covered in that class session. Polling can, however, be done with students before they learn a new lesson or mid-lesson as a way of reminding them of the key concepts they have learned so far, or immediately after completing a lesson as a way of testing their short-term memory.

Polling in Zoom

If you are using Zoom as a platform, this feature is available to you if you have an upgraded account. There are other platforms and tech tools that you can poll, but Zoom's feature is integrated, and students don't have to worry about linking to another website. However, if you don't have the Zoom polling feature, platforms like Polleverywhere and Mentimeter are easy-to-use options. Mentimeter was mentioned in chapter 2 for checking in with students, but this platform is multidimensional and can be used to create polls as well. When you use polling activities, you will get immediate feedback of where your students are at, what misconceptions they might have, what they value and what matters to them, and much more.

GREAT IDEA!

Gallery view game is a fun and low-stakes icebreaker!

Gallery View Game

One of the games we like to play with the students is called the Gallery View Game. This is an opportunity to ask questions to the students that might pertain to content or include questions that help students get to know each other and build community. For this activity to be successful, the students need to first turn off their cameras, then click in their settings to hide nonparticipants. Once a question is asked and if a student's response would be yes, then the student turns their camera back on.

To begin this question-and-answer session, we ask all students to make sure they are in the Gallery view (or something similar in whatever platform you are using) first (Figure 4.1).

Figure 4.1. Demonstration of how to choose Gallery view while you are in Zoom.

Once students are in Gallery view, they need to turn off their cameras. Then they scroll over anyone's name or picture and click on the three dots. Then click on the "Hide Non-video Participants option." You can hide everyone using this format or click on the video controls at the bottom and click it there.

As everyone completes this task, you included, there should be nothing on your screen except for your controls, but they can still hear you. If someone's picture or video is on, just tell them to turn their video off. Once everyone's camera is off and hiding nonparticipants, you explain to them that you will be asking them a series of questions. When the answer for them is *yes*, they are to turn on their cameras.

We use these five statements and go through them slowly to watch and see the results. Remember, you will read the statement first, then participants turn *on* their camera if the statement is true for them. If it's a false statement for them, they keep their camera *off*. These statements seem to elicit participation each time we do this activity as well as laughter, but they are also another way to find out some things about your students and build community in your virtual classroom:

1. You love a rainy day.
2. You love chocolate.
3. You tend to be critical of yourself.
4. You love to eat.
5. You have checked emails and social media during Zoom calls/classes. (This one *always* elicits a lot of laughter because *everyone* clicks on their camera!)

If you wanted to modify this activity by asking questions about content, you could ask them in a true/false manner. Another way to modify this activity is to use it to seek students' opinions: I thought that assignment was hard, or I didn't like working in a group, and so on.

Rename Game

While you are in your virtual session, you and your students can change your screen name in real time. But the "fun" begins when you ask the students to change their name to anything they want (I often do this in the beginning of the semester to get to know them). This could be a favorite actor, actress, singer, and so forth.

The easiest way to change the screen name is to scroll over your individual picture and click the three dots in the upper right-hand corner of your box. Once you do that, you will get a choice board for what you would like to do next, and you will click on rename. Then type in the name you want to appear on your box. Figure 4.2 describes these steps.

An activity that you could do is having students rename themselves to something relevant to your content. Then you could call on them to explain who they are and how it is relevant to the class topic. For instance, in a child psychology class, each student was able to select a childhood theorist of their choice and rename their box to that name. Then we went around the screen and had each student describe their theorist and what they knew about them.

Word of caution, be sure to change your name back or it will remain what is currently on your profile for your next Zoom or virtual meeting.

Figure 4.2. Steps to take to change names in Zoom.

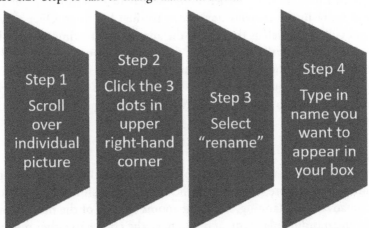

When you are in the physical classroom, it's very easy to ask questions and have students raise their hands to provide answers. There are normally students who always raise their hands, while some quieter students keep to themselves. Faculty have shared concerns that it is more difficult to get students to participate while in a virtual class, where students might be more hesitant to engage. The chat box, in whatever platform you are using, however, is a way to engage students, assess their learning, solicit quick feedback, and check in. You can support your students by actively using the chat box, where they can post questions and comments throughout your synchronous session. Faculty were able to see how those students who never spoke up in class were then participating in the chat.

A way to increase student engagement is using the chat box all throughout the class session. Let students know that your chat box is always open, and you will read the messages as you are able to. Invite students to the chat box so they can comment or question anything that comes up during the class. In addition to inviting them to the chat, you should also thank and acknowledge their chats. It's a way of building community and acknowledging their contributions.

GREAT IDEA!

Thank students for their chats to acknowledge their contributions!

Don't Touch the Enter Key!

Another activity to keep students engaged is to ask them questions and have them enter their answers in the chat box. The key here is to ask them to type their answers but not press enter until instructed to do so. This will give them ample time to type their answers without being pressured by the quick response of other students. When everyone has had a chance to get their response ready in the chat box, ask them to then hit enter. Once they do that, you will see as well as they do all the answers at one time. Then take a few seconds to review the answers that the students have given and let them scroll through them too. You can emphasize the correct answers, but you can also make use of the incorrect answers. You can ask the student(s) who wrote incorrect answers as to why they wrote what they did, and if they understand their mistake.

Breakout Rooms

Another example of a unique tool to make virtual classes more exciting and interactive are breakout rooms; however, successful breakout rooms hinge on advanced planning. Breakout rooms are one of the most popular features in an online platform, and you have the choice to either preassign each participant to a room, or randomly select students to a room, and/or have students self-select a room. When students are in smaller breakout groups, this tends to boost opportunities for students to share their ideas and interact with each other. Students will benefit from the direct interaction that they have with their peers within the small groups. This also builds social and cognitive presence as students interact with each other and the course content.

Google Forms

As stated in chapter 2, Google Forms provides an easy way to check in with students while also remaining private. To build those teacher–student relationships as well as strengthen their social-emotional health, Google Forms provides an effective way for faculty to check in and obtain information from their students. When used during a synchronous session, students will participate in real time, and you will be able to see their responses once they click the submit button. This could be used for a tool to elicit feedback from them on various items.

With Google Forms, you could create a series of questions and invite students to respond to those questions during a synchronous session. The application supports various types of questions like multiple-choice, text, paragraph, lists, checkboxes, scales, and grids. Responses from students can include entering free-form text, selecting from a scale, or choosing from a set of options. Once students submit their responses individually, Google Forms will tally the responses instantly so that you can share with the class on a shared screen.

When you create a Google Form, you can share the form through emailing each of the students individually or an easier way would be to provide the link in a chat box. Once each student accesses the Google Form, they can answer the questions individually, or you could place them in breakout groups to work on as a group assignment.

During this activity, students would be fully engaged since they would be required to submit their answers, and you could see who has submitted their responses once they have done so.

> **BIG IDEA!**
>
> *Using Google Forms can result in livelier class discussions!*

Once students complete their responses, you can show their answers on your screen. They can be kept confidential depending on how you share your screen and which answers you display. Once the answers are displayed, you could spend time discussing answers with the class (and have students

Figure 4.3. QR code to access a Google Form we created; click on "Make a Copy" to access.

verbally respond to any questions you have for them during the discussion or make use of the chat box). Using Google Forms in this way will provide interactivity between the students as well as between you and the students. This can result in longer periods of attention to the material being covered as well as a livelier class session. We provide a QR code to a Google Form template we created. You can click on "Make a Copy" and then you will be able to modify and use it (Figure 4.3).

In chapter 6, we discuss ways we use Google Forms for assessment purposes.

Part 2: Tips, Templates, and Tools

We provide the following tips on ways to support effective, engaging breakout rooms (Figure 4.4). We value the use of breakout rooms and the importance of students interacting with their peers and sharing content ideas in small groups. Finding time to incorporate breakout rooms into a synchronous session helps to engage learners and keep students actively participating:

Tips

Tips on Facilitating Effective Breakout Rooms

1. *Give explicit directions* before *they break out into groups.* You cannot share your screen to the whole class while they are in breakout rooms, so it's imperative that you provide the instructions of what you want them to do ahead of time. You can state the directions, as well as have them on some type of document that they will be working on (see number 2). You

Figure 4.4. Tips on facilitating effective breakout rooms.

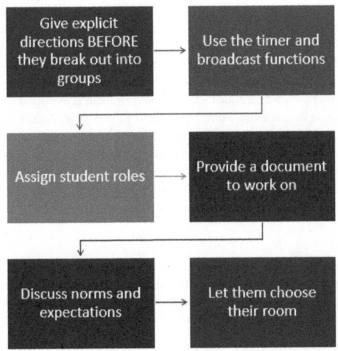

can encourage students to use the whiteboard function in Zoom while in their breakout rooms or work on a document.

2. *Provide a document that they will work on together during the breakout session.* This document can be a Google Doc or a Padlet or Jamboard so that they all can work on it collaboratively in real time. Word of caution, be sure to give each group a separate link to their particular document/ Padlet/Jamboard before they break out into groups. The chat box does *not* work during breakout sessions; however, there is a broadcast function that will send a message to *all* groups.

3. *Assign student roles.* Assign a *group leader* for each group as well as a *recorder*, regardless of if there is a document or Padlet/Jamboard that they're working on. This promotes ownership of the breakout room, and you as the facilitator can have one point person for each group. Plus, the group leader knows that you will be calling on them once the class is together again after the breakout session is over. Another role could be *timekeeper*, who will manage the time of the breakout session, as long as you use the timer feature as an option.

4. *Discuss norms and expectations ahead of time.* It's important to discuss with the students the "rules" of breakout rooms and what the expectations

are. This could be done collaboratively where they would state what they think the ground rules should be. Students would then be aware in advance of the expectations and what they need to contribute in a breakout room.

5. *Let them choose their breakout rooms.* A function in Zoom breakout rooms is "Let Participants Choose Room," where students self-select a room and you have predetermined which topic each room is to discuss when they arrive in that room. Students will be required to visit each room so that they can discuss each of the topics. This is basically a virtual gallery walk, where in the physical room, students would move from one Post-it poster to another which has a different topic written on each poster. Be sure to use the broadcast feature to keep students moving from one room to the next, as well as the timer feature.

Tools

There are many tools that are accessible and free to use to engage your students during a virtual class. In this section, we suggest using these tools for chatting during a virtual session, using an online whiteboard as well as a math specific whiteboard, and then finally making use of Jamboard.

Backchannel Chat

If Zoom isn't the platform that you use, but you want a chat room, there is a website that provides a free chat option for teachers and students. We share the chat box suggestions in Figure 4.5 that work in any platform where chat is utilized.

Backchannel Chat is one example of a chat tool we have used and there are free options available (http://backchannelchat.com). We provide a QR

Figure 4.5. Chat box suggestions that work in any platform that utilizes the chat function.

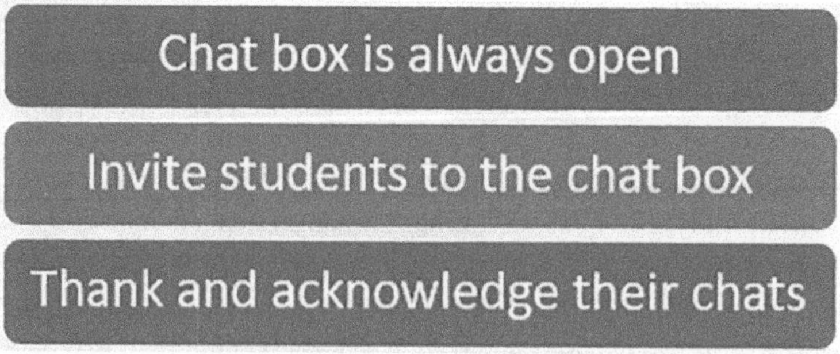

Chat box is always open

Invite students to the chat box

Thank and acknowledge their chats

Figure 4.6. QR code to scan to access Backchannel Chat.

code in Figure 4.6 you can scan to access this website and learn about this tool's background, purpose, functionality, and price options. Backchannel Chat provides a place where students and teachers can share text-based messages instantly. The chat is easy to set up and free for a teacher and 30 students or less. It can be used just like the Zoom chat by letting students ask and answer questions, and having class discussions and quick comprehension checks.

Online Whiteboards
Online whiteboards allow both teachers and students to share information in real time in a manner like how information might be presented on a whiteboard in the physical classroom. Zoom has an online whiteboard feature, but if you wanted students to have access to their own whiteboard, Whiteboard.fi is a good option.

Whiteboard.fi (https://whiteboard.fi) is a free online whiteboard tool for teachers and students (scan the QR code in Figure 4.7 to access). This interactive whiteboard can help you engage with your students and provides an opportunity for students to interact remotely. This website is a Kahoot! company and is user-friendly and engaging like Kahoot! Whiteboard.fi can be used instantly by creating a class and your students join by using a link, room code, or QR code. Everyone gets an individual digital whiteboard, where they can draw, write text, make notations on images, add math equations, and much more. You will be able to see your students' whiteboards in real time, so you are able to monitor and follow their progress, while the students only see their individual whiteboards and yours.

Figure 4.7. Scan QR code to access Whiteboard.fi

Whiteboard.fi provides instant access to your students because there are no registrations or logins needed. It will work on any device, so no installation or downloads are needed. It provides versatile tools for inserting images, backgrounds, arrows, shapes, and texts. You can ask a question in your synchronous session, and then let the whole class answer it by using Whiteboard.fi. When you ask a question in this format, you will activate the whole class and give everyone the opportunity to answer.

Jamboard

In chapter 2, Jamboard was discussed as a way of checking in on the students, and how to create one and use the controls. Jamboard is an interactive whiteboard that you can use to engage students with the material you are covering during your session. This digital whiteboard allows for remote collaboration on a shared space. If you lecture during your sessions, you could lecture for a time and then post up a Jamboard so that the students can interact with the material you just discussed. Students collaborate online in real time, but you share your screen so all the students can see what everyone else is doing.

BIG IDEA!

Always remind students how to use a tech tool even if it's not their first time using it!

Before the students are given the link to get into the Jamboard, we suggest explaining to them what they are going to do. Although you might use the same platform repeatedly during the semester, it is always helpful to explain the functions of the technology in case someone forgot. At the time of this publication, Jamboard does not assign the person's name to their work. So, to know who posted what, you can ask students to provide their name on each item they post. After sufficient time has been allotted, you can review everyone's answers aloud with the whole class.

Math Whiteboard

We wanted to mention a website called Math Whiteboard (https://www .mathwhiteboard.com/) and we provide a QR code to scan in Figure 4.8. Math Whiteboard is a collaborative whiteboard designed specifically for math teaching and learning. There are many functions to this virtual whiteboard which include a graphing calculator, the computer algebra system, writing or typing any math problems, and the ability to share the same collaborative math workspace with your students in real time by providing a link. It runs in any browser and works on any device.

The site even has example whiteboards that you can just click and use, for example, they have the following listed: slope intercept, math keyboard, animate rate of change, sine function, and quadratic relation.

Templates

We use Slides Mania to help us create engaging and interactive presentations for our synchronous sessions. We provide QR codes to access examples of templates from Slides Mania that can be used for a variety of disciplines. The medical template (Figure 4.9) could be appropriate for any medical course you might be teaching, the educational template (Figure 4.10) could be used in any course, and lastly the science template (Figure 4.11) could be used for any science course you are teaching. Once you are in the Slides

Figure 4.8. QR code to access Mathwhiteboard.com.

Figure 4.9. Scan QR code to access example of medical template.

Figure 4.10. Scan QR code to access example of education template.

Figure 4.11. Scan QR code to access example of science template.

Mania website, you will have access to a multitude of free PowerPoint and Google Slides templates. Take the time to browse through each of the categories to find the one(s) that you might be interested in using. Once you find a template you are interested in, follow the directions on how to easily download the template. Then you are ready to make them your own and customize the templates for your specific course.

Wrapping It Up

In chapter 4 we focused on ways to make your synchronous sessions engaging. We wrap up this chapter with the following points:

- Your role as a course designer and student engager begins with making use of your LMS, whether it be Canvas, Blackboard, etc. A list of best practices of using your LMS was provided.
- It's important early in the semester to establish clear routines and expectations. Review your LMS fundamentals so that the students will feel comfortable and be successful in your course when they are expected to use your LMS.
- You were given many different tips, tools, and templates to use as strategies to encourage engagement, participation, and accountability in your synchronous sessions. Using the suggested tools, you should be able to transform your synchronous session into an active learning community. One of the key factors in engaging students is making the content that students are learning relevant to their everyday lives.

BIG IDEA!

Create an environment that encourages participation and engagement with a predictable structure.

As noted in previous chapters, practice is key when adopting any of these tools. Additionally, it is critical that you create an environment that encourages participation and engagement with a predictable structure. Then, in chapter 5 we will focus on virtual instruction that is offered asynchronously, and how this type of offering online offers flexibility to both faculty and students.

Chapter 4 Reflection Questions

1. Is what we learned going to work with our learners? If not, then what do we do?
2. How can we support and advocate for our learners but also find ways to eliminate barriers and challenges and excuses that get in the way of virtual learning?
3. How can we use synchronous sessions to dig deeper and engage learners?
4. What tools work best during a synchronous session?

VIRTUAL INSTRUCTOR AS A CONTENT EXPERT AND A DIVERSITY, EQUITY, AND INCLUSION GUIDE

Using Asynchronous Instruction

I did then what I knew how to do. Now that I know better, I do better.

—Maya Angelou

Within this chapter, we focus on the roles of the virtual instructor as content expert and diversity, equity, and inclusion guide. Virtual environments are enhanced when learners can build content knowledge specifically with asynchronous instruction. Asynchronous instruction allows learners to engage with the content in the most effective and flexible ways that works for them and their schedules. In addition, we discuss in this chapter how asynchronous instruction helps increase cognition, remove educational barriers, and build social, teaching, and cognitive presence within a virtual environment. However, if learners are not able to engage with the content due to accessibility issues, this can impede the learning. We know how important it is for virtual instructors to be aware of issues such as diversity, equity, and inclusion and ensure that all learners can access, engage, and learn from this instruction. This chapter will support how asynchronous sessions allow flexibility and may provide greater access and diversity to our students when planned intentionally and thoughtfully.

Part 1: Virtual Instructor as Content Expert and Diversity, Equity, and Inclusion Guide

As we continue our journey toward becoming more effective virtual instructors, let us now turn to the role of virtual instructors as content experts and diversity, equity, and inclusion guides. We define *content experts* as individuals who are assigned to teach the course because of their research, experience, and/or skills related to the course content area. We stressed in chapter 1 that the virtual instructor is a facilitator of learning and how that role changes in a virtual environment. As content experts, the virtual instructor is expected to set up a classroom environment where learners can engage with the content and learn from this content. You can share your content expertise and build teaching and cognitive presence within your virtual classroom while preparing asynchronous sessions. In chapter 4, we focused on the virtual instructor as course designer and student engager and specifically discussed how to do this using synchronous sessions.

We believe, and stress throughout the book, the importance of incorporating both synchronous and asynchronous sessions, and the roles we discuss throughout the book can be and often are interchanged and applied in both asynchronous and synchronous settings. Within this chapter, we will focus on building content knowledge specifically with asynchronous instruction. We believe asynchronous instruction allows learners to engage with the content in the most effective and flexible ways and that asynchronous content presentation helps to increase cognition, remove educational barriers, and build social, teaching, and cognitive presence within a virtual environment.

And while you are building content within your virtual environment, you will also need to fill the role of *diversity, equity, and inclusion guide*. We define this role as someone who is aware of the diversity that exists within their students, intentionally embraces this diversity, and creates a virtual environment that is equitable and inclusive for all. We share ideas on how to ensure your course is accessible and how to use the principles of universal design of learning (Center for Applied Special Technology [CAST], 2018) to create this inclusive virtual environment.

Sharing Content Knowledge Asynchronously

As content experts, we must focus on ways to share our content knowledge in a virtual environment asynchronously, which brings important practices into play. We define asynchronous instruction as instruction that is offered to students at a time that works for them and not necessarily at the same time as the teaching occurs or at the same time with other learners. Virtual courses can include a combination of both asynchronous and synchronous instruction and there are benefits to offering both to learners. One of the main benefits of virtual teaching and learning is the flexibility that is offered to both faculty and students. From experience, we know that asynchronous teaching is different in many ways from synchronous teaching, and faculty and students need to understand the benefits and the challenges of this mode of delivering virtual instruction. We provide tools we have used to help us share content in an asynchronous environment.

In a study of postgraduate virtual students, the following themes were identified as causing barriers to self-directed learning in a virtual environment: cognitive barriers (overload of information, staying focused); communication barriers (understanding the role of student and teacher); and educational barriers (overwhelmed by the work and low coping skills; Kohan et al., 2017). Our goal in this chapter is to provide you, as content expert, with ways to use asynchronous instruction to help increase cognition, provide clear communication, and remove educational barriers so students can learn and thrive in your virtual classroom.

> **BIG IDEA!**
>
> *Asynchronous instruction is necessary in a virtual environment to reduce barriers for learners, increase cognition, and provide flexibility so learners can succeed.*

Increase Cognition With Asynchronous Instruction

Because learners may become overwhelmed with too much information presented at once, these suggestions are intended to help you to reduce cognitive overload, help learners stay focused, and increase cognition in your asynchronous learning environment. Working within your LMS (which should be capable of actions to a schedule), we suggest the following:

> **FACULTY PERSPECTIVES**
>
> *When faculty were asked what positives can come from virtual teaching, here are some responses:*
>
> *"Having to rethink how to do things. It is forcing me to change things up from what I usually do."*
> *"I get to learn new things and see where my past teaching could improve."*

- Set a time when the week or module will open automatically. For example, the module can be set to open at 7:00 a.m. on a Monday morning and then set up an announcement to go out at the same time to learners with a welcome to the week and information they should know about that specific week or module.

- Add a What Is Due chart to the course for each module or each week (see Table 5.1).
- Send out a weekly announcement (See Table 5.2).
- Provide a timeline for learners of when projects are due (these dates can be flexible). For example, you can give a final date when it must be submitted and a suggested date of when you would like it submitted.
- Create short videos of how to complete assessments or how to access a new technology tool with a screencasting tool such as Loom or Screencastify, or you can use your cell phone and create a video and post on YouTube for your students to watch. Your LMS may offer additional options to create this content, or you can embed the links within your LMS.
- Provide the resources learners should read each week, then, if desired, include additional resources they can access, if interested. This way, they know the resources they need to read and review to be successful, and they also have access to even more resources to continue or extend their learning.

TABLE 5.1
Sample of a What Is Due Chart Provided in the LMS for the Learners Each Module/Week

Monday	Thursday	Sunday
• Week opens 7:00 a.m. • Review course syllabus—contact instructor with any questions • Review overview presentation • Complete readings between Monday and Thursday • Watch all videos within the assignment section before completing assignments • Review all assignments in the Assignments folder	Add initial responses to the VoiceThread discussion	Respond to your classmates' posts by Sunday 11:00 p.m. Complete all assignments listed in the folder for this module: • Self-Assessment for Online Educator • Introductions—add to class Padlet • Flipgrid—What kind of teacher are you • VoiceThread Responses

TABLE 5.2
Sample Weekly Announcement

Hello everyone, I have enjoyed reviewing your recorded lessons over the break. I hope others get a chance to look in the folder to see what your classmates have done so you can get ideas from them.

For this week, there is a VoiceThread discussion. I have a VoiceThread that I shared in the lecture section of the course and then there is a different one in the assignment section. You only must respond to the one in the assignment section for credit. I have been taking a course on accessibility and am learning some interesting things. I tried out an app called otter.ai that transcribed me when I did the lecture so that I can easily provide the transcript to increase the accessibility of my course.

Here are some more resources I have gathered from the course and if they are helpful to you, please use them: Accessibility Resources; add to them as well if you have things to add.

Please contact me if you would like to set up a time to meet to discuss our course at any time.

The goal is to lower the cognitive load, help learners to focus on instruction, and provide scaffolding to increase cognition and skill acquisition.

Provide a Clear Communication and Feedback Plan
Because learners need to be more self-directed and the role of the teacher differs in an asynchronous setting, it is important to remove communication barriers by providing a clear communication and feedback plan. Sun and Chen (2016) shared that learners "want courses that are well designed and can enhance the possibilities for them to complete courses successfully, such as the clarity of the assignments and feedback that is consistent and timely" (pp. 166–167). We stress the importance of supporting students as self-directed learners (chapter 1), but as content experts, we have an obligation to design the course so learners can interact with course materials and know what to do to succeed and learn.

FACULTY PERSPECTIVES

Using the online platform, as opposed to face-to-face, has encouraged time management skills in the students.

There are various ways to keep them on track by sending them reminders, providing them with additional resources, and keeping things far more organized.

Proactive Communications

Communication needs to be frequent, clear, and provided in multiple ways. A welcome message for the course can provide information that can be helpful. We suggest providing a welcome message either in text or video that communicates to learners what they can expect from the course, how they will be interacting, and the best way for them to reach the instructor. The "What is Due" messages are also helpful for communication and can be shared in a variety of ways. We share another "What is Due" message (Figure 5.1) where learners can choose to attend a live session but if they are unable to attend, they can complete a VoiceThread assignment to receive credit. Because we are focusing on the flexibility and convenience that is offered in a virtual classroom, providing options and then ways for students to interact with content in flexible ways is always helpful, and communicating these options clearly is critical.

We suggest inviting learners each week to meet one-on-one via their video conferencing tool to clarify specific concerns or questions they may have. This is a reminder that can be set within the LMS in each module and then reinforced in announcements that are sent out to wrap up the week or module or to introduce the week or module, making it clear to the learners that although the instruction is asynchronous, you are still available to meet with them synchronously. This will increase teacher presence and reduce the feelings of anxiety or isolation that can arise from virtual teaching and learning.

BIG IDEA!

Asynchronous instruction provides a level of flexibility that can help increase access and support diversity and equity in your virtual courses.

Figure 5.1. Example of an announcement sent out to students in the beginning of the module. This "What Is Due" message can be used for both asynchronous and live sessions.

Monday	Thursday	Sunday
Begin reviewing material in Module 3 presentations; videos	Review and read all material in Module 3 by this date	Service Learning Activity #1 Completed and Submitted
Attend Live Session or Complete Alternate assignment which is Article Review	Begin reviewing material in Module 4	Review and Plan for PECT 3 exam - watch presentation
Plan for Service Learning activity #1	Finish planning service learning activity #1	Complete all activities in Modules 3 and 4

Feedback Planning

The OLC (2016) Quality Course Teaching and Instructional Practice score-card we discussed in chapter 1 consists partially of a student engagement component related to communication. This 15-point section of the score-card reinforces the need for effective communication that is meaningful and supportive. Feedback should be prompt, useful, and constructive, and students should know when to expect their feedback. In addition, we suggest providing feedback where learners can take the feedback, apply changes to their work, and resubmit to demonstrate their learning and growth. When learners know they are supported and they can learn from the feedback, they will be more prone to seek out the feedback and want to continue learning. Because providing this kind of substantial feedback to learners can be time-consuming, we suggest that using the following tools to provide asynchronous feedback:

- Flipgrid: You can provide feedback by video and audio that is person-alized and specific to each learner.
- VoiceThread: If students present their work in VoiceThread, it is easy to choose how you will respond with either voice, audio, or text.
- Use Loom or another screencasting tool to record personal feedback to the student while capturing your screen or for clarifying directions.
- The LMS where the work is submitted can be used by sending out announcements to all students and choosing the option for an email message to also be sent.
- Use a cloud tool such as Google Drive where comments can be made directly in the document.

BIG IDEA!

Feedback should be frequent, prompt, constructive, and allow students to make changes, if necessary, resubmit, and learn.

Identify and Remove Educational Barriers

To help learners succeed in an asynchronous environment, we know the importance of recognizing the diversity of learners and identifying and remov-ing educational barriers. If learners need support, they should be directed to the academic support resources available to them from the institution. Many institutions provide services but many times, especially if learners are in a virtual environment, they may not be aware of where to go for help. Also, by providing clear communication and lowering the cognitive load as we suggested previously, learners will be in a better position to learn. The flexibility offered by asynchronous sessions is also a way to remove educational barriers. If learners are not able to attend a live session and need to learn at a time or pace that works for them, then providing them with these options is critical. If a learner is not able to access an asynchronous session or lacks the technology to do so, instructors can create alternative ways for students to access the information and to learn. Suggestions that we provide on how to identify and remove educational barriers are as follows:

- Include frequent formative assessments built into the asynchronous sessions. We provide many ideas on how to do that throughout this book, but here are a few additional ways:
  - Create a Google Form with specific questions related to course content to check for understanding.
  - Use an add-on to Google Slides like Nearpod or Pear Deck and include polls, quizzes, open-ended questions, and reflective questions within the interactive presentation.
- Set up individual meetings with students if you notice they are falling behind, not present in the asynchronous class sessions, or not demonstrating the learning you are expecting.

GREAT IDEA!

Make some synchronous sessions optional and have asynchronous assignments learners can complete if they cannot attend live!

Building Presence in Asynchronous Instruction

As stated, virtual environments work best when there is a mix of asynchronous and synchronous instruction and where learners feel connected to the content, to each other, and to their instructor. One of the main challenges identified by faculty when it comes to virtual teaching and learning is their concern for the engagement of their students. We continue to refer to our chart of examples of social, teaching, and cognitive presence (community of inquiry framework; Garrison & Arbaugh, 2007). In Table 5.3, we italicized the specific examples we will cover in this chapter related to ways we can bring these presences into our asynchronous instruction. When asynchronous instruction is planned well, and the best tools are used to help this process, there are opportunities to build all three presences.

Building Social Presence in Asynchronous Virtual Instruction
Providing learners with opportunities to collaborate on assignments and/or assessments together is an excellent way to build social presence within

TABLE 5.3
Examples of Social, Teaching, and Cognitive Presence

Social Presence	Teaching Presence	Cognitive Presence
Getting to know other students	Getting to know the teacher	Making sense of the content
Expressing emotions and opinions	One-on-one meetings/ conversations with the teacher	Discussing the content for further understanding
Creating opportunities for collaboration	Asking the teacher questions	Digging deeper and taking part in project-based learning, service learning, research
Sharing a story	Engaging with teacher-directed assignments	Having students respond to other students
Building classroom community; supporting each other	Introducing a topic or project	Sharing knowledge and work with each other
Check-ins	Planning and preparing online course for student engagement	Providing peer feedback
Creating a sense of belonging	Creating an environment that is authentic and supportive	Using multimodal modes of instruction—videos, readings, resources

your asynchronous classroom. We provide many ideas on how to do this in chapter 3, but it is important to stress to students that there are multiple tools they can use to be able to work with others in the classroom on common goals but at different times (asynchronously). We also suggest modeling this by setting up a classroom environment that does just that. When we were writing this book, we created a Google folder and then folders for each of our chapters where we could see everything. We then created a timeline that we would follow to set deadlines for when each chapter would be completed. We had synchronous check-ins weekly at first, but toward the end of the project, we met synchronously almost every day. However, most of our collaboration was done asynchronously. We were able to balance our multiple roles and responsibilities such as providing faculty development, teaching, advising students, writing other articles, and so on. One of us even got married and was in Mexico for 3 weeks! The other planned and attended her son's wedding!

GREAT IDEA!

Build social presence in your course by creating collaborative assessments for your learners and suggest and model ways they can work asynchronously as well as synchronously if needed.

Building Teaching Presence in Asynchronous Instruction

In the asynchronous setting, the learners can have many opportunities to engage with teacher-directed assignments and content. Instructions presented in this way can help increase teaching presence by allowing the instructor to share content knowledge that can be accessed at the learner's convenience and pace. The learner can also rewatch, rewind, and skip through content to make the learning specific to their needs. Because many learners may experience cognitive overload as we discussed previously, this is also an opportunity for learners to decide when and how much of the instruction they watch at one time.

Also, learners want to know who their instructors are so providing them with a Padlet like the one we share in Figure 5.2 gives them an overview

Figure 5.2. Example of building teaching presence using Padlet and sharing the instructor's background, interests, and family with the goal of increasing teaching presence as well as social presence in a virtual environment.

of who their teacher is and helps to build this teaching presence in a virtual environment. You can see an example of this here: https://padlet.com/drmclaughlin/mystory. Sharing your research, projects you are working on, or articles or books you have written with your learners can also help to increase teaching presence. Students want to know their instructors are present in the course and that they are experts in their field. We also suggest including students in projects and research that you are actively working on. If there are community projects and initiatives in the area that you are involved in, this is also a good idea to share with your students so they too might be interested in joining efforts in improving their communities.

As noted previously, and the reason we have organized this chapter around asynchronous instruction, we have found that setting up the online environment for asynchronous instruction is an excellent way to demonstrate and build teaching presence and to share content knowledge. The online course can guide the learner through the content with teacher-created instruction that includes videos, documents, presentations, and graphics. When learners can clearly see what they need to do and when they need to complete it, and when the materials are created in such a way to engage the learners in deeper thinking and learning, teacher presence will grow. An organized and consistent setup

---

STUDENT PERSPECTIVES

When asked about their experience in an asynchronous course, students gave the following responses:

"provided prompt responses to emails and was never degrading or derogatory no matter how 'dumb' the question might have sounded. She was respectful and encouraging of the class and tried to provide us with many tools to use in our full-time jobs!"

"truly made this course engaging, relevant, and for current teaching professionals. Her expertise and her flexibility were truly appreciated, especially in the 'yo-yo' school year that is 2020. Her feedback was thorough, and expectations were clear."

"You always made yourself available if anyone had questions, you were so quick with giving feedback!"

"She made options available for us to choose the way we presented our learning and knowledge. She was flexible and supportive during the course when so many people are feeling stressed from COVID info and planning. She shared available resources for future reference and continued learning after the course."

Figure 5.3. Example of how a course is organized for learners—modules/weeks open one at a time and can only be seen after that date.

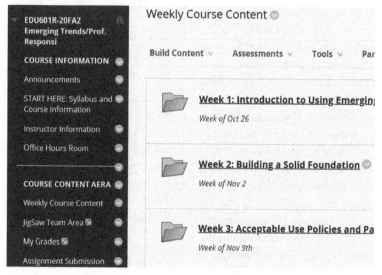

within your online course will create teacher presence and setting up modules to open gradually creates a sense of presence (Figure 5.3).

Building Cognitive Presence in Asynchronous Instruction

Instructor-led discussions can be embedded into a presentation using a tool such as VoiceThread, and then learners can use voice-recorded responses to share their experiences and reflections on their learning (McLaughlin et al., 2016). This type of asynchronous activity has been demonstrated to increase cognitive presence in a virtual environment. Providing learners with time to reflect on their learning and to hear their classmates' responses to their learning increases cognition and takes learners through the four phases of cognitive presence: understanding the purpose of their learning (triggering event); reflecting on their own values and beliefs (exploration); applying what they learned (integration); and putting it all together (resolution; Garrison and Arbaugh, 2007). Learners need time and opportunities to go through these levels of cognitive presence and this works best in an asynchronous environment because the timing and pace can best match the student's ability to process the input.

When students have opportunities to share work with each other and build on each other's work, this is also a way to increase cognitive presence in a virtual environment. We are fervent users and believers in cloud storage tools like Google Drive where learners can have access to the work even after the course is over. When students share their assignments not only with the instructor but also with each other, they can learn from each other. When peers interact with each other and comment and share ideas, this is also a way to increase cognitive presence. Discussion boards are a great way to do this as discussed in chapter 3, but only using discussion boards can prove to be repetitive and boring to students. You can diversify your virtual environments by using tools such as Flipgrid, Padlet, and Wakelet along with Google Drive and VoiceThread. New tools come out frequently and we suggest using the Evaluate the Tool template (introduced in chapter 1 and available in our Google resources folder) to evaluate whether a tool is the right one to use.

Creating an Equitable Environment

As a diversity, equity, and inclusion guide in your virtual classroom, asynchronous instruction can help you create a more equitable environment. Learners who may not be able to attend a live session due to life and work responsibilities or other barriers can still learn and thrive when provided with a flexible, yet robust virtual environment. The Peralta Community College District (2020) created an Online Equity Rubric that you can use to self-assess your course to see if your course considers diverse learners and provides a fair and equitable environment for all. Peralta College provides these resources for free, and they can be downloaded at https://web.peralta.edu/de/equity-initiative/equity/. The rubric provides a way for instructors to reflect on the following:

- What kind of technology supports and methods of accessing technology do students have? Is technology used in a way to amplify student voices and create an inclusive virtual community?
- Do students have access to support services or resources relevant to help them succeed in the course?
- Are the principles of universal design for learning evident in the course and are students given the opportunity to share their thoughts about this?
- Is diversity and inclusion evident within the course and are students given the opportunity to discuss diversity/inclusion? Are students and instructors aware of how embedding diversity and inclusion into courses improves learning?
- Are images and representations used in the course reflective of diversity and do students have opportunities to discuss these images and representations?
- Are there opportunities to discuss biases and how we need to be aware of our own biases?

- Are students able to connect course content to their own identities, backgrounds, and cultures and/or the identities, backgrounds, and cultures of others?
- Is there a sense of belonging and connection where students have opportunities to connect with others?

The Peralta Community College District (2020) offers a free Online Equity Training based on the eight rubric criteria. This training is free and provides an opportunity to learn about the criteria, analyze a sample course, and create your own materials to address diversity and equity in your own course. This training can be accessed at https://web.peralta.edu/de/equity-initiative/online-equity-training/ or you can scan the QR code (Figure 5.4).

Accessibility Tips

As virtual instructors, we know the importance of our role as a diversity, equity, and inclusion guide. We know that ensuring that our courses are accessible is an important component of this role. We are continually learning about ways to do this, and we offer the following suggestions to you as you set up your virtual environments:

- Using MS Word styles and templates helps to ensure the document is accessible.
- MS Word provides free accessibility templates for use; accessible templates from MS Office can be found at https://tinyurl.com/VISF-Ch5-1 or by scanning the QR code in Figure 5.5.

Figure 5.4. Scan QR code to access and download Peralta Community College Online Equity Rubric; this tool helps to self-assess the level of access and equity in your virtual environment.

Figure 5.5. Scan QR code to access accessible templates from MS Office.

- Web Content Accessibility Guidelines (https://tinyurl.com/VISF-Ch5-2; QR code Figure 5.6) were the most up-to-date guidelines for the past 20 years to use to make web content accessible and this comes from the World Wide Web Consortium (W3C).
- Web 2.1 (https://tinyurl.com/VISF-Ch5-3; Figure 5.7 [QR code]) was published in 2018 with additions that can be used with a smartphone or mobile device and complying with 2.1 will also comply with 2.0.
- Otter.ai (https://otter.ai/; QR code Figure 5.8) and Google recorder (https://recorder.withgoogle.com; QR code Figure 5.9) are free auto-transcribing tools that provide quick and easy ways to instantly transform audio into text. These tools allow you to transcribe your meetings, notes, and create accessible transcripts for voice-recorded materials.

Figure 5.6. Scan QR code to access Web Content Accessibility Guidelines.

Figure 5.7. Scan QR code to access Web 2.1 Web Content Accessibility Guidelines.

Figure 5.8. Scan QR code to access Otter.ai.

Figure 5.9. Scan QR code to access Google recorder.

- Provide learners with information related to disability services that are available to them in the beginning of the course, but also remind them of these services at different points throughout the course.
- Discuss with learners your desire to ensure the course is fully accessible to them and let them know they can come to you if they run into issues with accessibility. Sometimes it might be a simple change you can make to help the learner gain full accessibility or you may need the assistance and guidance of the office that specializes in disability services.

Evaluating the Tool

In this chapter, we will use the Evaluating the Tool (Table 5.4) template to evaluate using Pear Deck for providing asynchronous instruction to our virtual learners. Specifically, we use Pear Deck as an add-on in our Google Slides, but it can be used within Pear Deck itself.

GREAT IDEA!

Use templates and styles within MS Word to ensure accessibility within your virtual course!

Part 2: Tips, Tools, and Templates

The tips, tools and templates shared in this section are geared toward supporting virtual instructors as content experts as well as diversity, equity and inclusion guides.

Tips

The tips provided in this section focus on integrating universal design for learning principles within our virtual environments.

Universal Design for Learning

Universal design for learning (UDL; CAST, 2018) is a research-based framework used to create an inclusive environment. Research suggests that every learner's brain is different, and learners do not have one style of learning. For this reason, it is important to vary your teaching to meet the needs of your learners. Providing multiple modes of instruction not only meets UDL standards but builds cognitive presence as identified in Table 5.1. Asynchronous instruction is one way to meet the principles of UDL in a virtual environment.

CAST (2018) provides helpful resources on creating UDL environments. Rappolt-Schlichtmann (2020) shared multiple ways to integrate

TABLE 5.4

Evaluating the Tool

Name of Tool	Building Social Presence (list how)	Building Teaching Presence (list how)	Building Cognitive Presence (list how)	Tool is embedded in the LMS or has capability to be embedded into the LMS (Yes or No)	Format: Asynchronous Synchronous Face-to-Face Dual Learner
Pear Deck: https://www.peardeck.com/	Instructors can add slides that are specific to social-emotional presence and ask learners how they are feeling.	Instructors create the presentation and can share course content and information with the students and then provide the students with this information where students can respond either live during a synchronous session or asynchronously at a convenient time for them.	Learners have opportunities to make sense of the content when completing the Pear Deck activity. They can also reflect on their responses when they receive the takeaway document in Google documents that is generated after they complete the lesson.	Pear Deck can be added into the course LMS. It can also be, as mentioned previously, added on in Google slides.	Can be used both asynchronously and synchronously. For the purpose of this chapter, we will be using Pear Deck asynchronously.
Comments	Pear Deck is an easy way to make a lecture interactive. I have used Pear Deck both synchronously during a live session or asynchronously. When using it asynchronously, the learners interact with the content and respond to the slides. Then after all learners have completed the Pear Deck asynchronously, I can generate takeaways for each student. The takeaways allow the students to reflect on the presentation, add to it, and see the original responses they completed.				

Name of Tool	Building Social Presence (list how)	Building Teaching Presence (list how)	Building Cognitive Presence (list how)	Tool is embedded in the LMS or has capability to be embedded into the LMS (Yes or No)	Format: Asynchronous Synchronous Face-to-Face Dual Learner
Questions to Consider					
What organizational resources do you need to implement this tool?	The free version of Pear Deck allows anyone to make their presentation interactive; however, the paid version provides additional capabilities such as polling, takeaways, and the ability to have both student-paced or instructor-led presentations.				
What support do you need to use the tool besides an internet connection?	I currently pay out of pocket for the premium version of Pear Deck, but it would be helpful to have resources from my institution to cover costs of tools like this that make virtual instruction interactive.				
What is your backup plan if the tool does not work or does not accomplish what you thought it would?	Because Pear Deck is so user-friendly, I have not had problems with my students using this tool or even figuring out how to work this tool without much assistance. The only concern is the cost of it not being covered by the institution. NearPod is an alternative tool that can also make a lesson interactive and provide a good means of formative assessment data.				

UDL in distance learning including being clear on expectations, making materials accessible, using asynchronous instruction, and embracing the student as teacher. We build on these ideas and provide some additional tips to use UDL in your virtual environments:

- Make expectations clear; try using a hyperdoc like this Explain, Explore, and Apply Hyperdoc (copy and modify for use; HyperDocs LLC) found at https://tinyurl.com/VISF-hyperdoc (Figure 5.10–scan QR code).
- Provide a variety of ways for students to learn material (allow for choice with the Tic-Tac-Toe menu found at https://tinyurl.com/ vISF-tictactoe21; Figure 5.11–scan QR code).
- Allow for asynchronous learning (check out this Google Folder at https:// tinyurl.com/VISF-VT for ideas and examples for VoiceThread); this provides access and flexibility to learners (Figure 5.12–scan QR code).

Figure 5.10. Scan QR code to access HyperDocs LLC template.

Figure 5.11. Scan QR code to access template for Tic-Tac-Toe menu.

- Set up check-ins with your students—one-on-one Zoom meetings or allow them to sign up for one-on-one check-ins with When2meet (free tool to find a time to meet with a student; Figure 5.13–scan QR code).
- Keep communication open, which allows students to provide feedback—try an exit ticket created with Google forms at https://tinyurl.com/VISF-exitticket (Figure 5.14–scan QR code).

Another important way to improve your course using the UDL framework is to discuss this framework with your students and ask them ways you can create a course that they can access fully, learn deeply, and share their learning with others. Technology helps to create an environment that is inclusive by providing content in multiple ways. Ask students to suggest how they learn best and what technology tools they prefer.

Figure 5.12. Scan QR code to access examples of ways to use VoiceThread to support asynchronous learning.

Figure 5.13. Scan QR code to access When2meet.

Figure 5.14. Scan QR code to access example of an exit ticket made with Google Forms.

Tools

There are many tools that can be used to support an asynchronous, inclusive environment. We have found Pear Deck and Flipgrid (described in the following sections) to be helpful.

Pear Deck

Pear Deck can be used both synchronously and asynchronously. It can be used as an add-on in Google Chrome and provides opportunities for formative assessment, collaboration, higher order thinking, and active engagement of all learners. The free version allows you to ask questions and obtain quick formative assessments; the paid (premium) version allows users to draw, drag, and respond to polls. The instructor can also create student-led presentations as well as instructor-led presentations. The premium version also stores the data collected and creates individual takeaways of each learner's response. The learners can add to their takeaways with additional reflections and have their ideas to review and learn from. The instructor has access to this information as a formative assessment to determine whether content needs to be covered again or whether instruction can move forward to new content.

Pear Deck is easy to use and helps to make any presentation interactive. Pear Deck provides how-to videos that are short and user-friendly. You can type in https://www.PearDeck.com/help-videos or scan our QR code. Ditchthattextbook.com provides a multitude of tips on how to use Pear Deck and they also have templates you can copy and use. We created a QR code to take you to where this information is located (Figure 5.15). Ditchthattextbook also provides many other resources and we provide a QR code to quickly take you to this resource in Figure 5.16.

Figure 5.15. Scan this QR code to access how-to videos on Pear Deck.

Figure 5.16. Scan this QR code to access Ditchthattextbook.com and the many suggestions and resources they provide on using Pear Deck.

Flipgrid
This tool is perfect to use for asynchronous learning. Flipgrid is free and an engaging way to help learners share their ideas and have some fun while making video responses. Instead of asking students to speak in front of the class, this option allows students to plan what they are going to say, get their creative juices flowing, and improve in public speaking in the safety of their own home. All students can see and hear their classmates' responses and can also respond to their classmates. Instructors can provide written feedback and/or a video response in Flipgrid.

Google for Asynchronous Learning
Google is a great way to create an online collaborative and asynchronous environment for teaching online or face-to-face. Example of a folder created

for a course where learners can share resources, assignments, and collaborate with one another is EDU 603 (https://tinyurl.com/VISF-EDU603). The benefit of using a Google folder as opposed to storing everything in the LMS is that learners will still have access to the information after the course is over.

Students can submit their assignments in a shared Google folder or a similar cloud platform and provide peer review to each other on assignments. They can comment right in Google Drive to their peers. It also allows everyone to learn from each other, creates a collaborative classroom community, and promotes peer-to-peer support and interaction. Students can respond to their peers' assignments that are shared via links. Instructors can see and respond to the assignments and conversation as well. The students are able to divide efforts and research content, share with others, but then also learn from each other's work. Access to this information and learning does not go away after the course ends. Future students can also add to this work and benefit from the work of past students when collaborating within Google documents or a similar cloud-based tool.

Templates

We created a template, Online Learning Tools and Challenges (Table 5.5), that can be used to foster discussion and collaboration among colleagues on online learning tools you have tried and/or challenges you have had with these tools. The QR code (Figure 5.17) can be scanned where you can make a copy of this template and use it for your own reflection or with others to discuss. Feel free to adapt the template to meet your specific needs.

TABLE 5.5
Discussion Template for Online Learning Tools and Challenges

Online Learning Tools and Challenges
What and How
• What tools do you use or will use in your online course to engage your learners?
• How can you engage your students synchronously during your online course?
• In what ways can your students demonstrate learning (do not include tests or quizzes) in your online course?
• Any other questions that come up within your breakout group—please add.

Challenges
- What might stop you from trying or what resources/support do you need?
- What challenges do you have specifically with your course content and taking it online?

Be prepared to share with group

Breakout Group #1:

Favorite Tools/Engaging Students/Assessing Students	Challenges/ Resources	Comments

Breakout Group #2:

Favorite Tools/Engaging Students/Assessing Students	Challenges/ Resources	Comments

Figure 5.17. Scan QR code to access and use the Online Tool Template—feel free to copy, modify if needed, and use.

Wrapping It Up

Asynchronous instruction is an important component of virtual teaching and learning. As content experts, we can provide asynchronous instruction that increases access, removes barriers, and improves cognition and learning. Asynchronous instruction expands our ability to demonstrate content expertise through a range of knowledge pathways. And asynchronous instruction can provide students and faculty with time to process information more deeply and the flexibility to balance life and work responsibilities. Here are the key points discussed:

- Asynchronous sessions, when planned well, create opportunities for students to think deeply about the course content and provide a level of flexibility that is needed within a virtual environment.
- Talk with your students about ways to make your course as accessible as possible to them and be open to their suggestions. We can learn so much from our students.
- Find ways to embed discussions related to diversity and inclusion, no matter your course content, to ensure that all learners are included, and that diversity is valued and embraced within your course.
- Asynchronous instruction helps meet UDL by providing flexible ways for students to engage with the course content.

We hope you can use many of these ideas and encourage you to try at least one new way to flip your virtual classroom. Next, we cover the role of a virtual instructor as an assessor and project planner. We provide many ways you can engage your students with meaningful assessments. Trusting our students and leading them to self-directed, engaging, and flexible learning are always our goals.

Chapter 5 Reflection Questions

1. How can you use asynchronous instruction to engage your learners and help them become self-directed learners?
2. What are some different pathways students can use to gain access to the content?
3. How can you create a clear communication and feedback plan? What will be in your plan? How will you provide feedback asynchronously?
4. What does full access look like and how can every learner thrive in the virtual environment?
5. How can you make sure materials are accessible for all learners regarding technology issues and learning challenges? What accommodations do your learners need?

VIRTUAL INSTRUCTOR AS PROJECT PLANNER AND ASSESSOR

Assessment is today's means of modifying tomorrow's instruction.

—Carol Ann Tomlinson

I n this chapter, we focus on how virtual instructors can create environments that engage learners and assess their learning in creative and alternative ways. The virtual instructor is a project planner and an assessor. In virtual environments just like in any learning environment, assessment should drive our decisions and students need opportunities to showcase their learning. What works in an in-person environment is not always the best way to assess students in a virtual environment. We discuss authentic assessments and provide ideas to implement these assessments in a virtual environment. We also provide suggestions for using formative and summative assessments to engage and assess virtual learners in a virtual environment.

Part 1: Virtual Instructor as Project Planner and Assessor

We define the role of the virtual instructor as a *project planner and assessor* who plans and integrates assessments specifically that work within a virtual environment taking into account how this differs from traditional assessments in an in-person environment. The virtual instructor as project planner and assessor creates assessments where students are given opportunities to show what they know through alternative assessments, and we are not talking about tests and quizzes. The virtual instructor as project planner and assessor uses formative assessments to guide course decisions and summative

BIG IDEA!

Explain to students why they are doing a specific assessment.

assessments to assess program learning outcomes. The virtual instructor in this role integrates assessments that include choice, tying assessment to student learning and course outcomes, as well as allowing for creativity and innovation.

Starting With the Why

When creating assessments, you always want to first identify your learning goals and how these learning goals can best be accomplished in a virtual environment, what tools you might want to use to help accomplish these goals, and how students can demonstrate their learning to you. When you do give students an assessment, you can address the *why* of the assessment.

BIG IDEA!

Empower students to be designers in their own learning.

In the role of *virtual instructor as project planner*, you can explain to the students why it's important to know this information, and what they will do with this information after the class is over. To empower our students to be designers in their own learning, we need to provide opportunities for students to make choices and explore through authentic, engaging assessments. The projects you plan for your students and the assessments they complete will help to build cognitive presence within your virtual course. Examples in which carefully designed assessments can build cognitive presence are italicized in Table 6.1.

Planning and Using Authentic Assessments to Engage Virtual Learners

Planning authentic assessments in a virtual environment takes time and thought. We describe authentic assessments as assessments that provide learners with the opportunity to demonstrate their learning in a real-world setting. Some examples of authentic assessments include interviews, observations and reflections, performances and demonstrations, journals, and portfolios. eService learning is an excellent way for instructors to intentionally immerse students into learning that is engaging and connected to their course topic. Providing an option such as an eService learning project could help to remove barriers for learners who may not have the same access to take part in service unless it is offered in a virtual environment (Gasper-Hulvat,

TABLE 6.1
Examples of Social, Teaching, and Cognitive Presence

Social Presence	Teaching Presence	Cognitive Presence
Getting to know other students	Getting to know the teacher	*Making sense of the content*
Expressing emotions and opinions	One-on-one meetings/ conversations with the teacher	*Discussing the content for further understanding*
Creating opportunities for collaboration	Asking the teacher questions	*Digging deeper and taking part in project-based learning, service learning, research*
Sharing a story	Engaging with teacher-directed assignments	Having students respond to other students
Building classroom community; supporting each other	Introducing a topic or project	*Sharing knowledge and work with each other*
Check-ins	Planning and preparing online course for student engagement	Providing peer feedback
Creating a sense of belonging	*Creating an environment that is authentic and supportive*	Using multimodal modes of instruction—videos, readings, resources

2018). This project can also be used as an authentic assessment where learners can demonstrate the learning that took place during their service project.

Authentic assessments provide learners with ways to explore and demonstrate their learning in creative and engaging ways. We know from our research and our experience that traditional assessments, like quizzes and tests, are not as effective in virtual environments. We cannot

BIG IDEA!

Authentic assessments provide learners ways to demonstrate their knowledge.

continue assessing the same way in which we have always assessed as this will contribute to the frustration virtual learners and faculty will experience. We also know that giving students authentic and engaging assessments will help to decrease concerns with cheating and academic dishonesty. In addition, academic dishonesty increases when students are not clear of how they are being assessed or when they are under stress. We can lower this stress by providing learners with authentic assessments that are clear, connect to learning objectives, and provide flexibility and opportunities for collaboration and deeper learning (DeWitt, 2020). In real life, we have access to resources 24/7 to help us learn and attain knowledge. We should be able to use these resources as we demonstrate our learning in engaging ways. We can take cheating off the table when we rethink our assessments and find alternative ways for our learners to learn and demonstrate their learning. How many of us remember information we had to memorize and regurgitate in an exam or test? We typically remember the hands-on, engaging, authentic activities we participate in as learners. If we want to create engaging virtual environments, we need to think about everything we are doing and make changes where we need to make them. Figure 6.1 provides tips for planning assessments that increase learning, engage students, and support UDL principles. Stackable assessments can be used where students are given parts of their final assessment throughout their course, and these build up to their final assessment.

Figure 6.1. We want to create virtual assessments that build confidence in our students, help our students internalize their learning, and reduce risk, while also providing guidance and opportunities for collaboration.

Stackable and low-stakes
assessments . . . ***build confidence***

Project based and service-learning
assessments . . . ***internalize learning***

Work on final assessment from the
beginning . . . ***reduce risk and allow
for incremental guidance and
collaboration***

For example, if a student was taking part in a service-learning project, the stackable assessment could consist of the following:

Part 1: Write up a plan and goals for your service-learning project (where will you conduct your service, what do you hope to achieve, what questions do you have)—due in week 3.

Part 2: Interview someone in the field for whom you are providing service (e.g., if you are providing service for a crisis management hotline, interview the supervisor)—due in week 6.

Part 3: Conduct your service, document your service in reflective journals—complete hours between weeks 3 and 9.

Part 4: Synthesize your findings, reflect on your service, create a presentation, and share with peers and instructor—due in week 12.

Interview Assessments

Interview assessments provide opportunities for students to get out in the field, whatever their field of study is, and explore and talk to people who are leaders in the field. When students have opportunities to ask questions and see firsthand course concepts at work, this can help them engage deeper with the content. Another reason for implementing interview assessments is to open doors for students and help them to learn how to network as they will soon be looking for positions in the field. This assessment can be assigned in a virtual environment and students can ask for virtual interviews if meeting in person is not an option. We provide an example of an interview assessment (Figure 6.2) as well as the rubric we use to assess (Table 6.2). Students can share their completed presentations in a shared Google folder so others in the class can see the results. They can make

FACULTY PERSPECTIVES

"Initially I assessed using tests and quizzes, but the level of academic dishonesty is staggering. I am now assessing . . . through student-produced projects and lab reports on their own controlled experiments."

"Trying to ensure academic rigor and adherence to policies while also being flexible and understanding when students' circumstances force them to miss deadlines."

"Varying opportunities to respond—using chat, verbal responses, and various tech platforms to allow students to show understanding."

Figure 6.2. Example assessment that includes collaboration and opportunities to network.

Instructional Coaching Interview and Application: Instructional Coaching (50 points)

You will interview an instructional coach or someone who serves in the role of an instructional coach (principal, assistant principal, etc.) and inquire about the techniques they use to coach teachers. Review Aguilar's strategies and compare and share your findings. Within your writing, please describe how you would use these strategies and meet the needs of adult learners and research that supports this. You will present your research, key insights from your interview, and strategies you will use as an instructional coach. (Competency I and II)

Assignments should be placed in our Google Folder. Please review the Instructional Coaching Interview rubric.

Please note there is a peer review component of this assignment. You will review two other peers' presentations and submit comments, feedback, and suggestions within the Google Folder and you will receive credit for this per rubric.

---

their presentation interactive by using a tool like VoiceThread and others in the class as well as the instructor can make comments and interact with the material. Interview assessments also provide students with time away from technology if they are doing their interviews in person.

Service Learning

Service learning is an excellent way to intentionally engage students in learning that is authentic, tied directly to their content area, and can be done even in a virtual environment. Service learning would have to be set up in the beginning of a course with clear guidelines provided to students of what they need to do, why they are doing it, and how they can complete their service. Many campuses have experts who can guide and support you in integrating service learning into a course, especially if you are doing this for the first time. We recommend connecting with these experts and discussing the many components that need to be in place to do this successfully. One of the most important components in implementing service learning is institutional support and guidance as well as opportunities for students to discuss and reflect upon their service learning. There are many virtual volunteer opportunities students can find and being able to provide service and volunteer virtually can remove barriers such as access, resources, and disability. Students who may not easily be able to take part in a service-learning project face-to-face can do so in a virtual and accessible way.

If you are searching for an eService learning partner or place for your students to do some service virtually, we provide a few suggestions, but there are many more. We recommend looking for partners in your field and seeing how your students may be able to provide service virtually:

- Volunteer Match—https://www.volunteermatch.org/
- Create the Good—https://createthegood.aarp.org/

TABLE 6.2
Rubric Used for Interview Assessment

CATEGORY	4	3	2	1
Preparation (5 pts)	Research is extensive	Research is suitable	Research not suitable but shows some knowledge	Research shows little knowledge of topic
Interviewee (5 pts)	Person interviewed is extremely appropriate for topic	Person interviewed is appropriate for topic	Person interviewed is poor choice for this topic	Person interviewed is not an appropriate choice for this topic
Understanding of research—connection to course resources, text, etc. (15 pts)	Shows in-depth understanding of topic	Shows understanding but lacks depth	Shows basic understanding of topic	Shows little understanding of topic
Insights Gathered (15 pts)	Three or four underlying concepts presented and connected to interview	Two underlying concepts presented and connected to interview	One underlying concept presented and connected to interview	No underlying concepts presented and no connections to interview
Peer Reviews (10 pts)	Two or more comments to peers are thoughtful, useful, and provide suggestions or share insights	Two comments to peers are thoughtful but do not provide further insight or suggestions	1	0

- United Nations Online Volunteering—https://www.onlinevolunteering.org/en
- Crisis Text Line—https://www.crisistextline.org/become-a-volunteer/

Planning and Using Formative Assessments to Engage Virtual Learners

GREAT IDEA!

Provide students with eService learning opportunities where they can partner with virtual organizations that are related to the course content area and where they can have authentic opportunities to learn!

Formative assessments provide you, as assessor, with information about your students' learning, and how you can use the feedback to decide on the delivery of new content based on the results. It is used to check understanding of content, and then provide feedback and support to the students. But the feedback from the results of the assessment also provides rich information to the instructor as to whether students need more instruction or that they are ready to move on. As Angelo and Cross (1993) stated, the purpose of formative assessments is to improve the quality of the student learning.

BIG IDEA!

Exit tickets are a quick way to get feedback from your students and assess their learning.

Twitter Exit Tickets (Social Media Use) A quick and easy formative assessment to do with students are exit tickets. Exit tickets are quick, ungraded assessments that provide insight into students' learning. Exit tickets are questions that you ask the students to reflect on, based on the content delivered for that lesson, but exit tickets can provide feedback before the lesson, during the lesson, and/or after the lesson. Figure 6.3 describes how to design an exit ticket and provides an example of a simple question that could be asked, or one that is directly connected to the objectives of the class. The real value in using exit tickets is that students are engaged in the material that was just presented to them, which will transfer from short-term memory to long-term memory.

You will quickly see by their responses whether they met your learning objectives for that lesson. If they can respond easily with answers that reflect the content in the correct way, then you will know they have met your learning objective(s). Otherwise, if their answers don't correlate correctly, then you have a starting point for the beginning of your next lesson. As with any assessment, whether formative or summative, you should plan on being able to answer questions (Figure 6.4) as to what they will be learning (objectives), why they will be learning this (relevance), and how I will know if they learned it (assessment).

Figure 6.3. How to design an exit ticket.

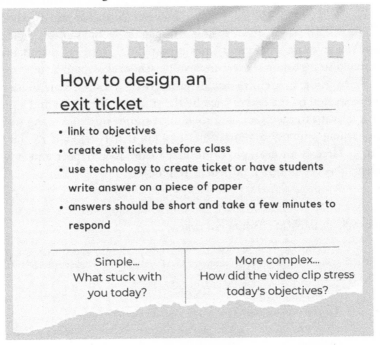

Figure 6.4. Assessment should answer these questions.

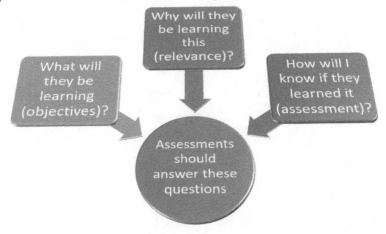

GREAT IDEA!

Make use of social media to post exit ticket questions and use hashtags to incorporate organizations on your topic.

To extend it further, make use of social media. In our classes, we use Twitter to post exit ticket questions, and then the students retweet and post their responses along with a class hashtag and any organizations that are relevant to course content; however, Snapchat and Facebook or Instagram would suffice. Figure 6.5 shows you an example of an exit ticket posted on Twitter that students had to respond to regarding the lecture on a preschool classroom layout.

When using Twitter, we usually post a tweet ahead of time so it's ready to be retweeted by the end of class by the students. We try to find a picture that is relevant to the tweet, and then ask a simple question along with the class hashtag and any organization's hashtag that is relevant to the topic (if any). Here is an example of an exit ticket Twitter post and how the students retweet and then post their responses:

Figure 6.5. Example of a Twitter exit ticket.

·Apr 7   ...

I found I had to be very careful of putting quiet and loud centers away from each other. #harcumedu228

Harcum College ECE @HarcumECE · Apr 7
#harcumedu228 What did you learn about classroom layout when doing this assignment?

Virtual Whiteboards

As mentioned in chapter 2, Whiteboard.fi offers a free online whiteboard tool for teachers and students. In chapter 2, we discussed how to use Whiteboard .fi as an engagement tool, but it also can be used as another formative assessment tool. When using it, it will provide you with live feedback and an immediate overview of your students' work. Students are more willing to try different strategies and participate in class activities when using virtual whiteboards. You can incorporate formative assessments using a virtual whiteboard by posting questions and having the students respond with words, images, videos, multimedia content, and so forth. Their understanding of the subject is seen through their posts. After posting a question, you will wait for the students' answers to appear on the virtual whiteboard. Whiteboarding, as it is commonly known, can be considered part of the learning process when using it for formative assessment purposes.

Virtual whiteboards provide immediate live feedback so that you can easily assess their progress in real time, but students can also assess themselves when comparing their responses to the others in the class.

STUDENT PERSPECTIVES

Here are some student perspectives when asked if the exit tickets/ Twitter posts and feedback help with their learning, which were very positive on this type of formative assessment:

"I was able to reflect on the class and look back at my tweets and be reminded of the content we had covered. A great tool for learning."
"The exit tickets help because they refresh my mind from what we learned in class that day.
It did even though I did not do all of them."

"Yes, because it was a way for me to understand what I got from the lesson."

BIG IDEA!

Virtual whiteboards provide immediate feedback.

On a side note, and an added benefit, since comments, annotations, pictures, and so on are viewed by all students in real time, students need to carefully consider the language they are using, plus ensure they can easily be understood by others in their post.

Another benefit of using virtual whiteboards is that they are effective tools for improving and accelerating literacy skills with students. These skills are ones that are needed in the workforce today, and again, this makes this type of activity relevant to the students.

Google Forms for Assessment

In chapters 2 and 4, we discussed using Google forms for checking in with students and engaging them during a synchronous session. It is a free online tool in the G Suite (Google Suite of Applications) that allows you to collect information easily, efficiently, and in real time. In chapter 6, we discuss using Google Forms to innovate your assessment practices. Google Forms is not a new tool; however, with its number of recent updates, it is a tool you can use for many assessment purposes. The Google form is set up the same way as in chapters 2 and 4 with a header (which will be discussed later in templates), and then questions are asked to students to check for their understanding on a topic.

One of the primary benefits of using Google Forms is its ability to help instructors assess how well students understand your material and what they don't, in real time. Once students submit their responses, you can see them immediately. With this timely system, you are able to adapt and change your lesson, if need be, for that particular class, or the next class.

Flipgrid for Assessment

Flipgrid is a simple, free, and accessible video tool that allows teachers to post a topic to a "grid," and then students post their videos to answer the question or respond to the topic. It is easily accessible using a Microsoft or Google account. Flipgrid works online so it can be accessed via web browser from nearly any device, or through the Flipgrid app, which makes it convenient for laptops, tablets, and/or smartphones.

The posted topic is essentially a video with some accompanying text. The idea behind this educational tool is to use video to create an open platform for discussion, which makes it very easy to get the whole class involved. Flipgrid is designed to allow students to speak to the whole group but without the fear of doing it in person. The video discussion platform helps educators see and hear from every student in class, which fosters a fun and supportive social virtual learning environment. Students can record their responses and post their video, which removes the pressure of answering in class in front of everyone. Since students are given time to respond when they're ready, it makes engagement possible with all students, even those who are more anxious and who might ordinarily feel left out in class, or those who might not participate otherwise.

Flipgrid is an app/website that allows teachers to create these things

BIG IDEA!

Have students use stickers and emojis in their Flipgrid post to promote creativity and self-expression.

called "grids" within the app to facilitate discussions. Students use the software's camera to create videos that are then posted to the topic. The benefit of using Flipgrid is that the videos can be recorded as many times as needed before the students upload. They can also add text, stickers, emojis, and drawings to their video. This encourages students to be creative and potentially more expressive in their responses. Students can engage with class content as they might interact with their friends using social media platforms like Instagram and Snapchat. Since Flipgrid parallels that of your students' favorite social media apps, this allows them to have fun while they are sharing their voice, as well as showing what they learned.

To use Flipgrid in the classroom, here is a link to access an easy-to-use guide by Fahey et al. (2019) that will walk you through the steps to set up your Flipgrid account and how to get started. On a software level, Flipgrid can easily be integrated into Canvas, Google Classroom, Microsoft Teams, and Remind. Figure 6.6 is the QR code to *The Educator's Guide* to Flipgrid eBook.

Polling in Virtual Classrooms
Polling in virtual classrooms provides many opportunities for teaching and learning, especially for assessment purposes. Polls are an efficient way to assess overall student understanding on a given topic, which can be done

GREAT IDEA!

Polls can be done before, during, and after your class session.

before a lesson, during a lesson, or after you are done presenting a lesson. Students are more apt to participate in a poll knowing that their answers are anonymous and low stakes. They are more likely to admit they don't know

Figure 6.6. QR code to *The Educator's Guide to Flipgrid* eBook.

something or freely pick an answer when they know the instructor doesn't know who answered what.

As stated in chapter 4, polling keeps learners alert and engaged throughout the lesson. It will break up the monotony of a lecture or looking at slides, and so forth. Polling not only breaks up the lesson, it also provides you with information that shows you how much students understand at any given point in your lesson. Polling is a nongraded formative assessment that can aid in preventing you from advancing in your lesson before students are prepared and ensures learners aren't left behind. Feedback from students at *any* time during the lesson is one of the best ways to make informed decisions about your lesson, and incorporating frequent polling is one of the best ways to accomplish this.

There are many different platforms of polling that can be used in the virtual classroom. Most are free to the end user, and some have limitations to the free version. The following are polling platforms that can be used:

Zoom polling—This is used within the Zoom platform.

Polleverywhere—Get instant audience feedback where no clickers are needed! This is a free polling platform where no signup is required. They offer multiple question formats such as multiple choice, true/false, word clouds, etc. Use the QR code (Figure 6.7) to access.

Mentimeter—Mentimeter was mentioned in chapter 2 for checking in with students, but this platform is multidimensional and can be used to create polls as well. Use the QR code in Figure 6.8 to access.

Figure 6.7. Scan QR code to access Polleverywhere.

Figure 6.8. Scan QR code to access Mentimeter.

Planning and Using Summative Assessments to Engage Virtual Learners

Planning and using summative assessments are also an important role of the virtual instructor. Summative assessments can help determine what students learned and how they applied that learning and whether program and course learning outcomes have been met. Part of the project planning is deciding what should be assessed and how the student learning will be measured. Miller (2020) suggested that these decisions on assessments should be strategic and focus on designing performance assessments where students can apply their learning. Summative assessments such as digital portfolios and end-of-semester capstone projects provide benefits that include increased cognition, real-world problem-solving, and developing communication skills (Newton-Calvert & Smith Arthur, 2020). We provide examples of summative assessments you can use in your virtual course.

Infographics as a Creative Assessment

An infographic (information graphic) is an attractive, professional, visual representation of data, information, or knowledge that can be used as an alternative assessment for an assignment. Graphics are used to represent complex information that needs to be explained quickly and clearly. Since infographics use a combination of images, words, and numbers, students have an opportunity to increase their effectiveness of communicating their mastery of knowledge.

Although the use of infographics in teaching and learning still appears to be an emerging practice, there are many benefits to using infographics for both formative and summative assessments. When students create infographics as their assessment, they are using technological literacy, visual literacy (finding meaning in imagery; Yenawine, 1991), as well as informational literacy. It is a way for students to creatively showcase their mastery of knowledge. Creating infographics is engaging; however, it is also a cognitively demanding task because students must represent the maximum amount of information within time and space constraints (Islamoglu et al., 2015).

BIG IDEA!

Infographics present the same information that has traditionally been displayed in posters or PowerPoint presentations, but in a current and attractive way.

Like oral presentations, infographics begin with an introduction to grab their audience's attention, and end with a conclusion so the audience can be left with an indication of what they could do with the information just learned (Islamoglu et al., 2015). If students choose to select this type of assessment to display their knowledge, it is a thought-provoking assessment. Students must visualize their idea, then explain their information in an eye-catching design. Infographics present the same information that has traditionally been displayed in posters or PowerPoint presentations, but in a current and attractive way.

Canva (https://www.canva.com/; access via QR code in Figure 6.9) is a platform that is easy to use to create infographics, but there are many others to choose from on the Internet. Figure 6.10 is an example of an infographic that was created for a social policy assignment in a child psychology course. Students were given a choice on how they were going to present

Figure 6.9. Scan QR code to access Canva.com.

Figure 6.10. Infographic example using Canva.

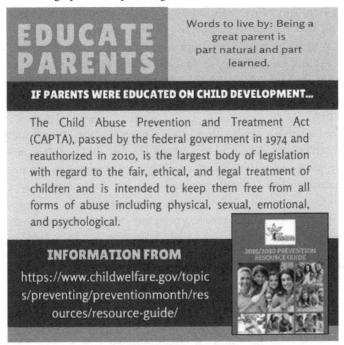

their selected social policy, such as a PowerPoint or Prezi, or an infographic. The infographic is compact, informative, and versatile in nature, and displays what the students know using textual information combined with graphical information.

3D Projects

When students have excessive amounts of photographs or diagrams to accurately describe a physical object for an assignment, students may benefit from using a 3D model for an assessment. While standard media types are crucial to the virtual learning experience, such as text, photographs, illustrations, and so on, a 3D model is another type with a lot of unique qualities (Loftin, 2018).

3D models are digital representations of physical objects, which could be an alternative way to display an image in the digital world. You might be thinking that 3D models would be too complicated to be of use in your courses, but that's not necessarily true. There probably isn't a day that goes by that you don't experience a 3D model in some way because they are *everywhere*! 3D models in digital form have been around for decades (Loftin, 2018).

There are many 3D model websites available all over the internet, where some are free, and others will require a fee. Students can search the internet to find what might work best for them, and which programs are user-friendly. Sketchfab (https://sketchfab.com/tags/education; scan QR code in Figure 6.11) and Free3D (https://free3d.com/; scan QR code in Figure 6.12) are websites that offer 3D models that are ready to view and download for free, and Record3D is an iPhone app that turns your mobile device into a 3D recorder.

A 3D model is a media object that has realistic depth and spatial presence and can be very impactful to students (Loftin, 2018). It is so much more than a simple photograph. When viewing a 3D model, you can manipulate it and examine it from all different angles.

One example where a 3D assessment was appropriate was where students were to design a preschool classroom layout using a program/website that would produce a computer-generated classroom. Students were not given

Figure 6.11. Scan QR code to access Sketchfab.

Figure 6.12. Scan QR code to access Free3D.

a particular website, because it was their choice on which program would best suit their needs. Making a 3D model allowed the students to be creative while solving a problem, and became one of their favorite assignments due to it being authentic and useful outside of the classroom.

Website or Blog Building

Students can be assigned creating a website or a blog for a summative assessment. There are many websites and blog-building tools such as Wix (www.wix.com; access via QR code in Figure 6.13) and Blogger (https://www.blogger.com; access via QR code in Figure 6.14). Both websites help the students create their own unique website or blog that is free and intuitive. It would be a way for students to showcase their knowledge in a unique way that they might be able to use in the real world, so this could be considered an authentic assessment as well as a summative assessment.

Free website creator tools often have ready-to-use design templates for students to work from. They offer quality starter templates that have easy drag-and-drop interfaces and plenty of creative control for students to make it their own. It makes building a website today easier than ever before. Students can easily add their own text and images and literally be up and running in minutes. This type of assessment is an opportunity for creative expression and content sharing, while remaining an authentic assessment due to it being relevant and useful in the real world.

STUDENT PERSPECTIVES

Student perspectives on which assignment they enjoyed the most during the one semester:

"The classroom layout was my favorite project. I really enjoyed doing it, and I feel like I gained valuable experience from it."

"I liked the preschool layout assignment because I knew about it early and wanted to get started on it. It was fun to create and presenting it was also fun. I enjoyed looking at all of my classmates' preschool classrooms because they were creative to look at."

"Doing a preschool layout helped me so much because I was able to see what really goes in a classroom."

Digital Portfolios

A digital portfolio is a way for a student to showcase all their best work from all their classes and add any relevant piece they feel passionate about. Digital portfolios should be intentionally embedded into the course from

Figure 6.13. Scan this QR code to begin exploring Wix.

Figure 6.14. Scan this QR code to begin exploring Blogger.

the beginning where students know what will need to be in their portfolios, when they will need to submit their portfolios (best to scaffold the submissions so they can build on their portfolio throughout the semester), and how this portfolio may be useful as they begin to search for employment in their field. Faculty can provide feedback throughout the semester on the portfolio so students can improve, reflect, and learn along the way. Students can collect, share, and showcase all their work in their personal professional portfolio using a tool such as Bulb (https://mybulb.com; access via QR code in Figure 6.15) or Squarespace.com (access via QR code in Figure 6.16). This is often used in the education world, but it can also be used for any job seeker to showcase their talents to a possible employer. These websites provide templates and examples for students to access so that they can create their own easily.

Figure 6.15. Scan QR code to explore Bulb.

Figure 6.16. Scan QR code to explore Squarespace.com.

End of the Semester Assessments

Giving students an opportunity to reflect on their learning at the end of the semester is a sure way to observe which information has been grounded into their long-term memory. Too often we feel overwhelmed at the end of the semester to cover the rest of the content that we need to, and then we forget all about our students trying to process all that information. According to Fournier (2019), cognitive load theory recognizes that overloading students with course content can impede their long-term processing of that information. So, with that in mind, instructors should just slow down and have students reflect on their learning and end the semester in a meaningful and effective way. The following activities are those that can be done at the end of the semester while taking a break from content:

1. *What Stuck?*—This written activity is one where students are asked, "What stuck with you this semester about this course?" Then students

reflect on their learning during the semester by summarizing content that they remember, and what they found valuable for their future employment.

2. *Writing a Letter to Future Students*—In this written activity, students will write a letter to future students who will take this same course. The students will inform the future students what they feel is the most important to do in order to be successful in this course. Students can write about you (the instructor), and how you are as an instructor, and how knowing this information can translate into success.

3. Taking #2 a step further . . . *Students Make a Video to Future Students*— Students are asked to create a short video introducing themselves and then explaining what they wrote in their letter to future students. A great way to house all of these videos is creating a grid in an app called Flipgrid.

   View an example of a Flipgrid video of a student expressing what they think future students need to do in this particular class: Flipgrid video to Future ECE Students (https://flipgrid.com/s/fddcb8d949b2) or scan the QR code in Figure 6.17.

4. *Gallery Walk*—This is an activity that is used often in a face-to-face course where there are sticky notes all around the room asking students various questions. In a virtual setting, and if on Zoom, you can use breakout rooms and assign each room a different question about the course. Once the students arrive in that breakout room, they complete a Google doc/ live document where they respond by typing their answers in real time.

5. *Review Game*—There are *many* platforms out there to have students play a review game of course content. You would create a review game of the

Figure 6.17. QR code to access an example of a student sharing their advice to future students.

most important items you want the students to retain, but make the game a low-stakes activity. Sometimes awarding the winner a few extra credit points is a huge incentive to students to try their best when playing the game. Games suggested to use are Kahoot!, Gimkit, and Quizizz.

6. *Review Padlet or Jamboard*—In this activity, students are instructed to place items (memes, words, GIFs, etc.) that reflect what they've learned in the course. Either platform is done in real time so that students can view what other students have posted. If using either platform, you would need to create the Jam or Padlet ahead of time and simply ask students to post items when instructed to do so. Then you review what each student has posted if the class is small enough or select ones if there are common themes.

7. *"Greatest Hits"* posts on a class blog or social media platform (Twitter, Facebook, Instagram, etc.)—In this activity, students reflect on their semester and can answer any of the following questions and post to the class blog or social media platform. Questions can be asked about things such as:
   - a funny moment from class
   - an assignment they are proud of
   - a funny "teacher X" moment
   - a post about a topic from class that they are passionate about
   - a great memory from the class
   - a post about something they learned that made an impact

8. *Letter to My Future Self*—This activity is really supposed to be completed in the beginning of the semester when you are setting up your safe virtual classroom. This is often done the first day of the semester, and we have great success in doing so. Students are asked to write a letter to their future selves. Some instructors ask students to write to their future selves about their hopes and fears, their predictions, their lessons learned, etc. Others will ask the students to write something to their future selves that is encouraging and uplifting for them to continue in their pursuit of a degree. We have done this activity with students, and it is amazing to see their faces when they read the letter at the end of the semester. This activity seems to always appear as a favorite on our teacher evaluations at the end of the semester.

   There is also another way to do this electronically by scheduling an email on Gmail. Another option is to use a website called FutureMe.Org (scan QR code in Figure 6.18) which will allow students to craft their own email and set a date to receive this email back, whether it's set for a 15-week timeframe, or 1 year, or 2 years, or whatever they wish!

Figure 6.18. QR code to access FutureMe.org.

9. *A to Z Reflection*—This is an easy way for the whole class to reflect on what they learned in a group setting. They must come up with a word or words that begin with each letter of the alphabet of something they learned this semester in your class. You could share your screen with a PowerPoint slide with each letter displayed that you could type on as they volunteer words *or* use a Jamboard where students can fill words in on their own. We prefer to have students talking instead of completing this activity on their own, so we usually share our screen and have them as a group go through the alphabet one at a time.

Providing Feedback on Assessments

Feedback has long been proven to be one of the most important factors to student success (Hattie & Timperley, 2007); however, many instructors fail to provide feedback on student assessments. After the assessment, students need to be given feedback. Here are some tips on how to provide constructive feedback so that the student will learn how close they are to the end goal.

BIG IDEA!

Feedback is the tool that can close the gap between where the students are and where you want them to be.

In conjunction with Nicol and Macfarlane-Dick (2006), the following list presents ways to provide feedback to students:

1. Write feedback that is *specific* to what they did correctly and where they need to improve. Don't use the phrase, "Good job," and think this is

feedback. Students need to know *what* they did a good job on, and why you thought it was good. How does it align with the expectations in a rubric?

2. Feedback must be *timely*; comments need to be returned to students quickly after an assessment. Students often complain that instructors take too long to return assessments, and then they forget what they did originally.

3. Feedback should tell them how to *reach the ultimate goal*, which Hattie and Timperley (2007) referred to as "feed forward." Your feedback should explain what they can do to reach the end goal and how to get there. It closes the gap between current and desired performance (see Figure 6.19).

4. *Don't use a red pen!* Even when grading "papers" virtually, don't use the red marker in your LMS. Research has shown that when instructors use a red pen of some sort to grade papers, students find this to be negative

Figure 6.19. Cycle of feedback on assessments.

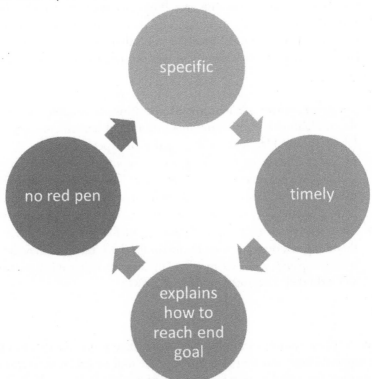

regardless of if they did well. Students become anxious when they see lots of red marks on their paper, even if the feedback is positive. So, use a different color; perhaps use a color that is a school color. Thankfully at one of our colleges, the school color was purple!

Part II: Tips, Tools, and Templates to Support the Virtual Instructor as Project Planner and Assessor

Within this section, we provide tips, tools, and templates to support your role as a project planner and assessor in the virtual environment.

Virtual Assessment Tips

While working with faculty, we have seen the most frustration come about when they were trying to assess the same way they have always assessed, but in a virtual format. We know from experience and from our research that mimicking a face-to-face assessment in a virtual environment will not be a good experience for the faculty or the learner. This is a great time to rethink your assessments and try something new. If our goal is to help students learn, we need to use tools and practices that help them to do this effectively and then find ways to have them demonstrate what they have learned in creative ways. This chapter provides many ideas you can try, and we leave you with the following tips:

- *Trust your students*—When you take cheating off the table and provide the students with authentic and meaningful assessments, they will (almost always) learn and will exceed your expectations.
- *Do not be afraid to try something new*—Keeping that mindset of taking a calculated risk and not being afraid to fail will help when trying something new. Because virtual environments constrain us, this is a perfect opportunity to change your practice and assess in a new way.
- *Allow students to resubmit and redo*—Students will learn more when they are given opportunities to obtain feedback on what they did not quite grasp and, with coaching and mentoring, being able to resubmit and redo their assessment will show growth.

Tools

There are many features within learning management systems that can help us to support virtual learning assessments. The tool we focus on in this section is using the quiz feature of your LMS to explain assignments to learners, ensuring they are reviewing important information ahead of time, and providing their acknowledgement of reviewing what is expected in their assessment.

Using LMS Quiz Function to Explain Assignments

How do you typically tell students your expectations for an assignment virtually? Do you write them down in a separate document, review them orally during a session, and then field repeated questions throughout the semester? Most likely you do, but what about making use of your LMS quiz function to walk students through assignment expectations step-by-step as another means of communication?

You would create the quiz by first listing out the components of the assignment in a bullet list. Then have students affirmatively answer questions about the different components with a simple "Yes, I understand" or choosing between options. You will see an example of one of the questions that was used in an educational psychology class in Figure 6.20.

GREAT IDEA!

Use your LMS Quiz function to explain the parts of an assignment.

Figure 6.20. LMS quiz function to chunk assignment expectations.

Question 1	1 pts

Assignment Components

- Research topic and completion of worksheet
- 2 articles from professional journals, citations (APA format), synopsis of articles
- Follow 2 organizations on Twitter, post a tweet that supports your social policy
- Write a letter to your PA State representative explaining why you want them to support your social policy
- Present your findings in your choice of media

What must you do while researching your topic on the Internet?

○ complete a worksheet

○ write down 3 items

○ I don't know

With this method, it chunks expectations and paces students through with frequent small questions. Chunking refers to an approach for making use of short-term memory by grouping information together. These chunks are easier to commit to memory than longer information that is easy to forget. By separating information into chunks, it becomes easier to retain and recall. The Peak Performance Center (2021) described the benefits of chunking: it "facilitates comprehension and retrieval of information" (para. 7). Virtual learners can be supported when chunking is implemented and they are able to process the information in smaller amounts.

Templates

The template we provide is a Google form that we have used as a formative assessment. It can be modified and used for any content area and used either asynchronously or synchronously. This template was used during a synchronous session where learners were asked to complete a quick assessment to check for understanding and to see how the learners felt about the lesson and how they felt about an upcoming assignment.

Google Forms for Assessment Template

To access the example of the Google Form Assessment template (https://tinyurl.com/VISF-Ch6-1), use the following link and/or the QR code in Figure 6.21. When you access the template, you will need to click on Make a Copy. You will then be able to modify and change the form to meet your needs.

Figure 6.21. QR code for Google Assessment template.

Wrapping It Up

In the role of virtual instructor as a project planner and assessor, you can design and implement many of the ideas offered in this chapter to create engaging virtual environments. Using a combination of formative and summative assessments that work well within a virtual environment will help your students learn. We offer the following suggestions:

- Provide students with meaningful projects and opportunities to demonstrate their learning using a combination of formative and summative assessments.
- Move away from traditional quizzes and tests and think of more creative ways to assess your learners.
- Ask your learners for suggestions on ways they can demonstrate their learning.
- Trust your students by taking the concern of cheating off the table by giving them opportunities to collaborate on assessments, use resources available to them, and use feedback given to them to redo or rework assessments so they learn.

In the next chapter, we will be wrapping up our book and discussing ways to continue to learn and grow when it comes to virtual teaching and learning, and we stress the need to take care of yourself, your wellness, and look out for each other. Intentionally connecting with others and collaborating on ways to improve virtual teaching and learning can help manage the uncertainty that comes with trying new things!

Chapter 6 Reflection Questions

1. In what ways have you changed your assessments when teaching in a virtual environment?
2. How can we take away the problem of cheating and provide our students with high-quality ways to demonstrate their learning?
3. What is an appropriate authentic assessment you can try in your virtual classroom?
4. What challenges have you encountered while transitioning your assessments to work in a virtual environment?

7

VIRTUAL INSTRUCTOR AS A LIFELONG LEARNER AND KNOWLEDGE SHARER

You don't have to see the whole staircase, just take the first step.

—Martin Luther King, Jr.

This chapter focuses on the role of the virtual instructor as a lifelong learner and knowledge sharer. As we continue to grow as virtual instructors, our tool choices and resources will grow as well. We know the learning never ends as we continue to refine our skills as virtual instructors. Virtual learning and teaching can help us to collaborate with others, have access to information easier and be able to share this information with others easier. Virtual environments can increase our flexibility and provide our learners with the same flexibility and access. We provide suggestions on ways we continue to learn and share with each other and others.

Virtual Instructor as Lifelong Learner and Knowledge Sharer

As we come to this final chapter in our book, we want to focus on faculty in the role of lifelong learner and knowledge sharer, because we know there is so much more for us to learn, explore, and share related to virtual teaching and learning. We define the role of a *lifelong learner* as someone who is always looking for ways to improve their practice through research and experience. We define the role of a *knowledge sharer* as someone who not only continues to learn but continues to share their learning with others. As much as our focus in this book has been on student learning and engagement, we know from our own experience and our research that there is always something new for us to learn and for us to share with others. We have reiterated the importance of focusing on the learning and not on the specific tools, because new tools are plentiful. We stressed the importance of building mindsets that embrace virtual teaching and learning (chapter 1) and the value of finding a team to collaborate with (chapter 3). We know all the roles we discussed throughout this book are interchangeable and are not sequential, and we respect and value the time and energy that all of you have put into creating engaging virtual environments and the many roles you fill throughout this process. We also know how hard this work is and the need for taking care of ourselves, mentally and physically.

The current trajectory of the teaching and learning landscape includes the need for virtual learning and new ways of offering courses to students whether it be asynchronous or synchronous classes. As colleges and universities now rise to the challenge of embracing new models of course offerings to students, we will evaluate what is worth keeping in the virtual classroom and define what authentic student engagement looks like in synchronous and asynchronous sessions, as well as what assessments are appropriate in this setting, and how students can thrive socially and emotionally.

How should institutions of higher education proceed with virtual learning? What virtual tools and technologies should be considered as they navigate this new landscape? What should students expect in the future with intentional virtual class offerings? Postpandemic virtual offerings must move beyond the traditional way instruction is delivered; instruction is not just about covering content and reading PowerPoint slides. Instruction should be student-centered where student engagement is key and not an outdated delivery method of just lecturing and feeding information to the students. Students should not be taught the same way we were taught. We need to evolve teaching and learning from being transactional to now being transformational. Kilpatrick et al. (2021) said it well: "In higher education, we will want to learn from and continue any adaptations or innovations that were beneficial, so that we can continue to improve teaching practice" (para. 1). We agree with this statement wholeheartedly and we encourage you to continue learning and growing and trying new things.

FACULTY PERSPECTIVES

"I just will seek the opportunity to continue to be creative with my approach to the learning journey."

"I have found the students to be helpful and flexible."

Continual Improvement of Student Engagement in Virtual Environments

Although most faculty and students were initially overwhelmed by their relocation into virtual environments during the pandemic without adequate training or preparation, we now can focus on high-quality online environments, which would include all the items discussed in previous chapters using the OLC (2016) scorecards, the Evaluating the Tool template, and other tips, tools, and templates provided throughout this book. Forward-thinking faculty can focus on their preparation of offering a quality virtual class, which will include many different engaging tools. We know that when students are engaged in high-impact practices and provided a virtual environment that is flexible, thought-provoking, and research-based, they will thrive. We have learned that being aware of our students' mental and socioemotional health is also of utmost importance. We shared a multitude of ways to do this during your virtual teaching, whether you choose to do this asynchronously and/or synchronously—we recommend checking in with your students in a variety of ways and frequently throughout the course of the semester.

The number one concern of faculty we work with and talk with continues to be student engagement. Many of the tips, tools, and templates we discussed within this book provide ways to measure and heighten student engagement. We know new technologies are coming out all the time and we recommend that you use the Evaluate the Tool template to discuss the tool and decide which ones are best to use and why. Asking colleagues what tools work best for them is also a good way to find something new.

Faculty Lifelong Learning and Professional Development

We all need continual professional development opportunities, so we are well-equipped to redesign and improve our courses. This is an exciting opportunity to transform virtual teaching and learning and to see what is possible with proper use and training in technology. Many times, we will grapple with the rapid technological advancements taking place, but this is progress toward creating quality virtual courses.

Professional development is about continuing and refining pedagogy; it is a process rather than an outcome. As a dedicated educator, you know that professional development yields many benefits. We also know that faculty, as adult learners, want professional development that is meaningful, that they can apply immediately, and where they can contribute their own ideas and experiences. We value the faculty and student perspectives that we have gathered throughout this process, and we plan to continue reaching out to faculty and students to continue offering support and resources. We offer at the end of this chapter a link where you can continue to share your voice, your ideas, and your stories with us. Keep telling us, keep sharing with us, and we will continue to look for opportunities to highlight your perspectives.

We believe faculty development works best when faculty choose the topics they will be learning about and when faculty have time to discuss and share ideas with each other.

We continue to believe the best way for us to learn is to learn together and while we are amid figuring things out and learning ourselves. Therefore, the mindsets we discussed in chapter 1 are of utmost importance. We need to be comfortable with taking a risk especially when we are not certain of the outcome. We need to be flexible with our students, with each other, and most of all with ourselves. All the tips and tools dis-

FACULTY PERSPECTIVES

"I'm grateful for everything provided and the fact that we survived!"

This faculty member shared the following: "Online format worked well for most students. Consistency across instructors and programs would have been helpful but everyone was learning how to teach on the fly, so it is totally understandable that there were some inconsistencies and differences."

"I am grateful for Covid in that it has allowed me to open several doors to new teaching modalities and I plan to incorporate them when we are fully in person. With that being said, I can't wait to be back in person."

cussed within this book can be used in multiple environments, although we are specifically discussing and targeting virtual environments. However, these tools and activities can engage learners whether they are in-person, virtual, or in a dual learning environment.

Faculty Book Club/Book Studies

There are many benefits of joining a faculty book club if your institution hosts one, and if they do not, you could start one! Book clubs/book studies offer professional development opportunities for faculty when they are involved with reading and coming together to discuss and to reflect on the selected book among other faculty members. Participation in a faculty book club/study provides opportunities to examine educational issues as well as offer suggestions on pedagogy and how to improve the practice of teaching and learning in a nonthreatening way.

FACULTY PERSPECTIVES

"Workshops and opportunities to collaborate with and learn from colleagues."

"More time, more PD that was meaningful and could be implemented immediately."
"More professional development to learn the tech tools and how to use them."

"Hoping our institution will take time to hear from faculty and to process this experience once it is over."

FACULTY PERSPECTIVES

"It reminded me how important my relationships with my students are. When they are struggling and come to me for help, I have to come up with an action plan to meet their individual needs. Once it is implemented and I start to see they are truly understanding the material, it is an amazing feeling."

"To see a student feel good about themselves and take pride in doing the work to achieve success is one of the best parts of being a teacher."

"That great teachers inspire their students to reach higher in learning."

At our institutions, we were fortunate enough to benefit from the generosity of our administrators who saw the benefits in providing the books/eBooks to our faculty who wanted to read the books, for which they incurred all costs associated with reading the books. The administrators saw how faculty who were actively involved with the book club were expressing how this was a great alternative to professional development. Most see professional development as a mandate from administrators which lacks relevance. If faculty members are invested in their professional development, they will find opportunities that will be relevant to their practice.

Book clubs/studies provide a social and intellectual forum for teachers to share their thoughts, ideas, feelings, and reactions (Flood & Lapp, 1994). The goals for faculty book clubs/studies are to provide teachers with the opportunities to examine their knowledge, beliefs, and practices through reading about alternate perspectives (George, 2002). The benefits include the introduction of new ideas for their teaching, it encourages teachers to take ownership of their ideas, and it provides opportunities to dialogue and compare perspectives (Burbank et al., 2010).

One of our selections was *What Great Teachers Do Differently* by Todd Whitaker, and the faculty were asked if they had any takeaways from the book, and their responses are shared on this page.

Faculty were also asked what they like about the book club and why they attended. Their responses indicated their desire to collaborate and hear the ideas of their colleagues. Book club also provided faculty members with an opportunity to get to know each other and interact with faculty in different departments and disciplines.

Informal Sharing Sessions

While working with faculty, we have found so much value in providing space for informal sharing sessions. In one of our institutions, we were working on strategic goals in our school, and were assigned teams to work with. One of the goals was finding ways to collaborate and share strategies for online teaching and learning. This team began holding open sessions where faculty could join via a virtual meeting and either share what they were doing in their virtual classrooms and/or obtain ideas from others on tools or strategies they were trying. This collaborative informal sharing was stress-free, supportive, and low key, something we all needed during a stressful semester. Sometimes the members of the team would share specific ideas of what they were trying, or they would listen and relax like the others in the group. It was a self-directed, supportive sharing session—one that we all desperately needed. Although being assigned to a strategic goal does not sound all

"To respond first with empathy—I'm sorry that happened to you."

"Don't say to a student, 'This was great, but'. . . If you are going to give praise, just give praise. Don't taint it with a 'But' statement."

"Prevention versus Revenge and High Expectations. Setting these in place from the very beginning set the stage for a successful semester. Establishing trust is important, as is self-reflection and course correction when you make a mistake."

FACULTY PERSPECTIVES

"I really enjoy hearing everyone's thoughts and reactions and getting to know some newer faculty members I may not know too well yet."

"I just wish we had more time to talk about the books and even maybe follow up on ways we implemented the ideas, what happened, what we discovered, etc."

"It was good to hear other people's views about using tech or not, and how that might affect how I continue to expand my use of tech in the classroom. Thank you! Book Club is going very well. Each meeting is better than the last one."

that fun, it was amazing to find this time where we could support each other and share with each other.

Virtual Classroom Visits

We believe not only do our students benefit from peer support, but so do we as faculty members. Inviting a peer into your virtual classroom is a good way to receive feedback and advice in a nonthreatening way. We suggest finding someone you trust and connect with and asking them to walk through your virtual classroom and then offer to do the same for them. This classroom walkthrough should be for the sole purpose of seeing what is going well, reflecting on how to grow, and getting ideas from each other. Preplanning is always a good idea, so we suggest the following:

- Decide on what specifically you would like someone to look at when they visit the classroom. Are they looking at the course content and how the course is set up? Are they looking at the interaction between students, instructor, and content? Is there one specific area of the OLC scorecards you might want them to look at? We like these scorecards to help guide our discussion and reflection as we improve and grow as virtual instructors. The more specific you are, the better your feedback will be.
- Decide on a mode of where and how the information will be shared—will you share a Google document? Will you have a video call to debrief?
- Will you plan a follow-up walkthrough, discussion, collaboration? How will you use the information you gather?

GREAT IDEA!

Invite a peer into your virtual classroom and ask them to provide you with helpful feedback as they walk through your virtual classroom.

Be open to ways to make things better and pick someone you trust!

Teacher's Mental Health and Well-Being

We want to stress the importance of being aware of mental health and well-being and acknowledge that we know virtual teaching and learning can be challenging and can feel overwhelming at times. We also know that it can be rewarding and open doors for students to have greater access and hopefully greater learning and provide more flexibility and tools for faculty to use to engage their students.

Ways to Maintain Your Mental Health

Our favorite faculty quote from the previous list is "The social and emotional impact on everyone is off the charts." We agree and know that more than ever, it is important to maintain your own mental health. We added some tips throughout the book related to mindfulness and socioemotional check-ins for this very reason. As we move forward and venture into more virtual teaching and learning, we want you to always take time to take care of yourself. If something is too much, talk to someone. We know that as faculty, we may be expected to hold things together, but it is okay to ask for help, say no if you need to for requests of your time, and take breaks. We also know that academia can be isolating and competitive, but it does not have to be, which is why we suggest ways to find your team in chapter 3. We know how important it is to have a support system within your work environments.

FACULTY PERSPECTIVES

"Administrative; PDs on topics we want to learn about; something for the teachers' mental health and wellness, not just the students' mental health and wellness."

"Faculty have been stretched incredibly thin. I feel as if a lot of information was thrown at faculty regarding online teaching. Could there have been more understanding about challenges faced by faculty and, perhaps, reduced responsibilities so that faculty could have had more time to develop their online teaching skills?"

"I would have liked more wellness check-ins for mental health and support."

"The social and emotional impact on everyone is off the charts."

We suggest the following tips and things that we do to reduce our stress and help with our mental health and wellness:

- Read a book that is not related to your teaching—if reading is something you enjoy doing but have trouble finding the time to do. We know this is hard to do, so if starting or joining a current book club helps, do that. If joining a book club would only add to your stress, do not do that!

- Step away from the technology—you do not have to be available 24/7 to your students or to your work. You deserve and need downtime. We are not so good at taking our own advice, but we know this is important. Sometimes virtual environments make us feel like we do not have a start and end time for working since we can work anytime and anywhere.
- Flexibility is great, but sometimes you need to set boundaries; don't be afraid to set them. And they are your boundaries, so you can change them anytime you want. Do what works best for you.
- Ask for help—do not be afraid to tell someone you need help. There are so many people who care and want to help—let them.

Sharing Resources

As much as we want to be able to help ourselves and others when it comes to mental health and wellness, many of us are not professionals or trained in this specific area. We recommend having a list of resources available to share with your students and your colleagues or anyone who may come to you who may be struggling and need more than the previous suggestions we shared.

- Check for your institution's resources related to counseling and mental health for both employees and students. Have this information available and handy if you need it. Virtual environments may mask specific needs a student may have but having check-ins and one-on-one meetings with students will help.
- If there are concerns related to safety, the suicide prevention lifeline is available 24/7 at https://suicidepreventionlifeline.org/ or 1-800-273-8255.

Stressing the Importance of Checking on Socioemotional Wellness

We know the importance of making sure students know their mental health is more important than school and that their mental health and well-being is of utmost importance to you. We spoke about the importance of checking on students and each other's socioemotional health throughout this book, but we provide an example of how to begin a virtual synchronous class and ask students to respond. Faculty meetings can also be started with a virtual prompt like this to encourage everyone to think about the individuals and the stress they may be under and the support they may need.

Zoom Fatigue

We know how difficult and draining it can be to be in one virtual environment after another. We know that fatigue from this experience is real. We also know that faculty (and students) are burnt out by the end of a semester, but the beautiful thing about that is that we can recharge, reenergize, and refuel! We are very aware of the need for rest and relaxation once the semester ends, but once

BRIGHT IDEA!

Faculty are used to knowing what they are doing, but virtual learning is completely different and can cause frustration and stress—acknowledge this, talk about it, and seek help when and if you need it.

you are ready to look toward the next semester, you will be ready to go with all of the tips, tools, and templates that are in this book. Suggestions on taking a break from the screen are throughout the book—and we highlight a few of them as follows:

- In chapter 6, we provide many examples of assessments that can be done away from the Zoom screen such as authentic and high-impact assessments.
- In chapter 5, we discuss how to flip the classroom instruction and include more asynchronous opportunities for learning which allows for a break from the screen as well as flexibility and accessibility to students.
- Giving students choices on how they demonstrate their learning can also provide a break from the screen.
- Limit synchronous sessions and ensure that synchronous sessions are interactive and engaging.
- Allow students to turn off cameras and interact using a tool like Pear Deck or NearPod.

Listening and Learning From Faculty Voices

We asked faculty on multiple occasions what they needed after a year of virtual teaching and learning. Many of the responses included something related to time. They needed more time to absorb the content, more time to collaborate with one another, and more time to try new things. Building in time for faculty to do these many things is a critical part of helping them succeed and grow in teaching and learning in a virtual environment. As faculty members, we suggest advocating for this time and stressing the importance of collaborating with colleagues and having the support of administration to try out new ways of teaching and learning. We created a summary of other needs identified by faculty. We know this list is not inclusive of all the needs, but we are constantly on the lookout for ways to help our faculty and colleagues thrive in a virtual environment:

- What is up and coming related to online teaching and learning?
- Faculty need access to a variety of resources—where can they be found? Faculty and learners need technology that is up to date; tools that work within the LMS are preferred.
- Faculty need support from administration—emotionally, financially, and with time/resources.
  - Faculty need subscriptions for virtual tools and should not have to pay out of pocket for these—free versions are limited.
  - Faculty need professional development, money to be in courses, and opportunities to collaborate.
- There should be more check-ins on socioemotional wellness—this is hard and can be isolating. You may think faculty have it all together, but we need support too.
- Faculty require flexibility from colleagues, students, and administration.
- Support for learners—what do our learners need? How can we support them emotionally, financially, and with time/resources so they can be successful?

Someone suggested the need for catch-up days and we can also call them curriculum enrichment days or weeks where faculty and/or students do not have new work assigned or modules to review but can take time to catch up. We believe these opportunities should and can be embedded into our syllabi and courses so faculty and students can breathe and have opportunities for reflecting on their teaching and learning.

Conclusion

As we navigate through virtual learning postpandemic, we hope that our book has given you many ideas on how to create the ultimate learning environment whether you host synchronous or asynchronous classes. Our book is like no other higher ed book because it is a how-to book with step-by-step instructions on how to create items to make your virtual environment an engaging one. There aren't other how-to higher ed books; most how-to books are saved for the K–12 world. We welcome opportunities for continued collaboration. We have created a Google folder where resources are shared, and we would be happy to include resources and ideas you have to share as well.

Figure 7.1. Scan this QR code to access our Online Teaching Resources Google folder.

Please reach out to us and we will collaborate on adding to the content. We also know that virtual technologies constantly change, but the foundation of what makes virtual teaching and learning engaging is built on ways in which you build community and social presence within your virtual environments, integrate teaching presence and cognitive presence into your asynchronous or synchronous classrooms, find a team to collaborate and learn with, and develop your ability to have a growth mindset and embrace the habits of mind we discussed in chapter 1.

Online Teaching Resources Google Folder

Our Online Teaching Resources Google folder can be accessed by scanning the QR code in Figure 7.1 or going to https://tinyurl.com/VISF-folder to collaborate and share ideas with each other. Just as we stress in the book, we need to support each other, and we can do this all virtually! We plan to update the folders and encourage you to share items you would like to see in the folder or ideas you would like to share with us. The idea is to make this a collaborative, growing resource for those of us working hard to engage our virtual learners. We can do this so much better together. Our learning and sharing does not have to end once this book is finished!

Tips, Tools, and Technology to Support the Virtual Lifelong Learner and Knowledge Sharer

Within this section, we provide tips, tools and technology to support you in your role of virtual instructor as a lifelong learner and one who collaborates and shares knowledge with others.

Tips on Virtual Classroom Visits

Classroom observations can be a key strategy to improving teaching and learning, provided they are conducted in an appropriate manner. To improve your practice as an online instructor, try to observe other instructors while they are teaching a course. By observing others in the virtual classroom, you may be able to identify gaps in your own practice and then improve your teaching with the ideas you get from the observations.

Virtual walkthroughs can provide clear, actionable feedback about how you are doing in your course when comparing your practice to someone else's. The following is a list of tips when doing virtual classroom visits to make them more effective:

1. Emphasize self-reflection—Virtual walkthroughs that are conducted well will promote self-reflection at multiple levels. As you observe, self-reflect on your own practice compared to what you observe. Think about the strengths and weaknesses of your own practice.
2. Identify gaps in practice—When preparing for your virtual walkthrough, think of the areas you feel you need to improve, then design your walkthrough around that. What do you need to see in the walkthrough to help you address the gap(s) in your practice?
3. Select instructors outside of your discipline—When selecting instructors to observe, try to observe ones from all disciplines and not just your own. See how other instructors conduct a class from the start of class, while they lecture, what activities they do to engage their students, and then how they end their class. By observing other instructors outside of your own discipline, it will give you a different perspective of how content is delivered to the students.
4. Create a community of feedback—Discuss before and after an observation with the instructor about their class session. Ask them questions about how they implement the certain aspects of their lesson, and possible suggestions on how to improve your practice.
5. Observe another instructor's course in the LMS—Ask if they can share their course in the LMS so you are able to see how they curate and create instructional materials, tools, strategies, and resources to engage their students and to ensure academic success.

Tools

Social media is an excellent way to stay abreast of what is going on in our field. It is a way to share knowledge with others as well as gain knowledge.

Social Media Use

What does your institution use for social media platforms? Twitter, Facebook, Instagram, Indeed, YouTube? If your institution has a center for teaching and learning, which may be named something along those lines, you should make use of all of the social media platforms it uses to stay connected for news, updates, workshops, events, and so on.

In addition to making use of your institution's social media, you could also find many resources using a Twitter account. If you haven't already created an account, by all means, create your free account today! You don't even have to use your real name; name it something that is unique to you.

You might be skeptical and thinking, why should I use another social media platform like Twitter? What could I possibly benefit from using it? Well, there are lots of benefits from using Twitter, because it is a powerful educational tool that has the potential to support teaching and learning! We are going to highlight just some of the benefits of using Twitter to benefit yourself in the higher education world. Twitter is a tool that allows you to connect with other educational professionals, as well as expand your personal learning network, otherwise known as your PLN.

One of the ways to make Twitter work for you is to find "your people." As the education world becomes more digital, instructors have more and more opportunities to connect with each other, as well as the organizations that support their discipline. Most likely when you sign up for this account, you're going to first start following people you know; however, Twitter isn't the platform to post pictures of yourself or post personal things like you would on Facebook and Instagram. Instead, use the search bar and search topics that you are interested in. For instance, if you are teaching psychology, you might want to search that term and see what results are yielded. The search results will show you accounts of people who have listed that term in their profiles, so they would be the first ones to start following. Your results will also show specific tweets containing that term. Click on the profiles of the people or organizations that tweeted and see if they would be a good connection for you. If they are, then start following them too. Again, Twitter isn't like Facebook and Instagram where it would seem creepy if someone that you don't know starts following you or you start following them. Once you start following these people and organizations, you can interact with them or just obtain resources from their tweets.

Many people equate Twitter with professional development because it is a platform to obtain resources and share resources. Every time we go onto Twitter, we wind up discovering something new, obtain a new resource, find out about a conference, and so forth in just a few minutes. It has become our practice to check Twitter every day, and sometimes several times a day. Our professional knowledge is enriched by what we find on Twitter.

Templates

The template we share in this section can be copied, modified and used to support virtual classroom peer observation. There is so much we can learn from visiting and discussing our virtual teaching and learning with our colleagues.

Virtual Classroom Peer Observation Template

This Virtual Classroom Peer Observation template can help support a positive peer observation in your virtual classroom (Figure 7.2). The tips throughout the chapter and book stress finding someone you trust and connect with to team up with and provide each other feedback and support.

You can access the Virtual Classroom Peer Observation template at https://tinyurl.com/EVL-peerobservation and make a copy of it and use it or scan the QR code in Figure 7.3.

Figure 7.2. Example of a template to be used to conduct peer observations.

Virtual Classroom Peer Observation Template
Goal: Sole purpose of this observation is to identify what is going well, reflecting on ways to grow, and gaining ideas from each other. Any other goals you want to include:

Preplanning Stage
Identify with your peer what areas you want to focus on (areas to consider: course design, learner engagement, interaction between learners and learners, instructor and learner, learner and course content):

How will this information be shared (video feedback, in-person session, Zoom session, shared document)?

During the Observation
Notes:

Follow-Up Actions

Figure 7.3. Scan QR code to access Virtual Classroom Peer Observation Template.

Wrapping It Up

In the role of virtual instructor as a lifelong learner and knowledge sharer, you were offered suggestions on how to continue your professional development as well as maintain your mental health. We wrap up this chapter with the following key points:

- Your role as a lifelong learner should include ways to learn professionally through participation in professional development workshops and conferences, but also events and activities your institution provides like book club/book studies and informal sharing sessions.
- Part of being a professional is to take care of yourself and your mental health.
- As a knowledge sharer, you can share your knowledge in many ways. Book club/book studies are some ways but sharing resources with other instructors is another way to share, and it can be done in different formats.
- Twitter is a way to share your knowledge, but also a platform for professional development where you can do research and connect with others who share your same professional interests. It's also a way to connect to organizations that are connected with your discipline, where resources can be shared.
- Be your own advocate to express the support and resources needed to perform your job well as an instructor.

Chapter 7 Reflection Questions

1. How do we stay current on virtual learning and best practices?
2. What can we take with us into our virtual environments to create more engaging, flexible environments?
3. How can we reduce video fatigue for our students and ourselves?
4. How can we advocate for ourselves and our students for the resources and support that we need?

T hroughout this book, we discuss multiple tools that we use and that we have found to be helpful in creating engaging virtual environments. We know tools change all the time and because of this, we stress the importance of focusing on the learning and not the tool. However, we also know that as virtual instructors we can benefit from sharing ideas with each other and suggestions on tools to try. Sometimes we mention the same tool in multiple chapters, and this guide will help identify when and where we talk about specific tools. We also provide additional supports and resources within our Google folder and will update this folder as we continue learning and experimenting and engaging our learners in the virtual environment.

Tool Description	References	QR Code
Backchannel Chat http://backchannelchat.com/ Class discussion tool that allows for safe and secure online discussions—free version for teacher and up to 30 students.	chapter 4	
Bitmoji https://www.bitmoji.com/ Create your own personal emoji to use in your virtual classroom or other apps/email.	chapter 2	
Blogger https://www.blogger.com/ Create a blog—it is free and easy to use, and there are templates to help you get started.	chapter 6	

(Continues)

Tool Description	References	QR Code
Bulb https://my.bulbapp.com/ Learners can create digital portfolios to showcase and share their work. There is a free version that allows for 10 portfolio pages.	chapter 6	
Canva https://www.canva.com/ Create professional documents using the templates and graphics provided and add collaborators for group projects. There is a free version for individuals and small team collaboration.	chapter 2	
Capitalize My Title—Zoom Backgrounds for Teachers https://capitalizemytitle.com/zoom-backgrounds-for-teachers/ Find free Zoom backgrounds to add to your virtual classroom.	chapter 2	
Classroomscreen.com https://classroomscreen.com/ Create a landing page for your synchronous class where you can personalize the learning and stimulate student engagement. There are free options available.	chapter 2	
Discord https://discord.com/ Free backchannel chat options where learners can chat and share ideas with each other.	chapter 3	

Tool Description	References	QR Code
Ditchthattextbook https://ditchthattextbook.com/ Free teaching ideas, templates, blogs—great resources to use right away in your own virtual classroom.	chapter 3	
Flipgrid https://info.flipgrid.com/ Simple and free video discussions to make learning fun and engaging. Great way to have students introduce and get to know each other in a virtual environment.	chapters 1, 5, 6	
Free3D https://free3d.com/ Create free 3D models to use as assessments and ways to make learning come alive.	chapter 6	
FutureMe.org https://www.futureme.org/ Learners can write a letter to themselves, to other students who may take the course in the future, to the instructor, etc.	chapter 6	
Gimkit https://www.gimkit.com/ Create review games, live games for synchronous sessions, and asynchronous assignments for learners. There is a 30-day free trial.	chapter 6	

(*Continues*)

Tool Description	References	QR Code
Google Drive https://www.google.com/drive/ Free cloud storage where learners can share ideas and collaborate—course folders can be created and shared so learning does not have to end when the course is over.	chapters 1, 3, 5	
Google Forms https://www.google.com/forms/about/ Create free online surveys/assessments.	chapters 2, 4, 6	
Google Jamboard https://jamboard.google.com/ Create, collaborate, and bring your learner's ideas together in a shared jamboard.	chapters 1, 2, 4, 6	
Google Recorder https://recorder.withgoogle.com/ Transform audio into text to support an accessible virtual environment.	chapter 5	
iMovie https://apps.apple.com/us/app/imovie/id377298193 A video editing tool developed by Apple that can be used to turn videos into movies. This can be used to create course trailer videos or for learners to showcase their learning.	chapter 2	

Tool Description	References	QR Code
Kahoot! https://kahoot.com/schools-u/ Create engaging trivia games that can be played live with small groups or self-paced and asynchronously.	chapter 6	
Loom https://www.loom.com/ Easy-to-use screencasting tool to capture your screen and share videos with learners. There is a free version for educators.	chapter 1, 5	
Math Whiteboard https://www.mathwhiteboard.com/ A collaborative whiteboard designed specifically for math teaching and learning.	chapter 4	
Mentimeter https://www.mentimeter.com/ Create interactive presentations that embed quiz questions and polls.	chapters 2, 4, 6	
Nearpod https://nearpod.com/ Can be used to create interactive lessons with games, videos, activities. Nearpod offers both synchronous and asynchronous options and can be added on to Google slides to make a Google slides presentation interactive.	chapters 5, 7	

(*Continued*)

Tool Description	References	QR Code
Otter.ai https://otter.ai/ Free tool to transcribe voice conversations into notes to make them instantly accessible. There is a version specific for education. When presenting, Otter.ai can be automatically turned on to begin transcribing.	chapter 5	
Padlet https://padlet.com/ Padlet is an interactive digital bulletin board where learners can share videos, audio, text, links, and collaborate with each other. There is a free version.	chapters 1, 2, 5, 6	
Pear Deck https://www.peardeck.com/ This tool can be integrated and added on to Google slides to make presentations interactive, informative, and fun. There are templates available to help support an engaging, active virtual classroom environment. Presentations can be either student-led or teacher-directed so they can work in both asynchronous or synchronous learning environments.	chapters 5, 7	
Polleverywhere https://www.polleverywhere.com/ Engage learners instantly with polls, surveys, Q&A sessions, word clouds.	chapters 4, 6	

Tool Description	References	QR Code
Powtoon https://www.powtoon.com/ Animated video creation tool that learners and teachers can use to seamlessly share teaching and learning in an engaging and fun manner.	chapter 1	
Prezi https://prezi.com/ Presentation tool that is easy to use; it is engaging and free for students and teachers.	chapter 1	
QR code generator—GoQR.me https://goqr.me/ There are multiple free QR code generators. This one is easy to use and you can create instant QR codes to integrate into your virtual classroom.	chapter 2	
Quick Rubric https://www.quickrubric.com/ Create quick rubrics using this website and share the rubrics with your learners.	chapter 3	
Quizizz https://quizizz.com/ Find and create quizzes and lessons to engage your learners.	chapter 6	

(Continues)

Tool Description	References	QR Code
Rubistar http://rubistar.4teachers.org/ This website assists in creating quick, effective rubrics to use in your virtual environment.	chapter 3	
Rubric Maker https://rubric-maker.com/ We know how important it is to create effective assessments with rubrics that are easy and quick to make.	chapter 3	
Screencastify https://www.screencastify.com/ Easily record, edit, and share videos. This free tool can be added on to Google Chrome.	chapters 1, 2, 5	
Sketchfab https://sketchfab.com/tags/education This website offers free 3D models for download and use.	chapter 6	
Slack https://slack.com/ This tool provides a backchannel method to communicate with students and for students to communicate with each other. There is a free version to try.	chapter 3	
Slides Mania https://slidesmania.com/ Free presentation templates for PowerPoint and Google Slides—options to create a choice board and/or interactive presentations.	chapters 2, 4	

Tool Description	References	QR Code
Socrative https://www.socrative.com/ Stimulate higher learning with higher order thinking questions and engage students in on-the-fly assessments.	chapter 3	
Squarespace https://www.squarespace.com/websites/create-a-portfolio/ Showcase and share student work via this online digital portfolio.	chapter 6	
Trello https://trello.com/ This free project management tool helps teams work on projects and collaborate.	chapter 3	
Twitter https://twitter.com/ This free social media tool can provide opportunities for students to share their learning and connect with other professionals in the field. It can also be used as a backchannel to discuss course content.	chapter 6	
VoiceThread https://voicethread.com/ Create interactive multimedia slides to which you can add voice-recorded comments and where learners can collaborate, share, and interact with their instructor and each other.	chapters 1, 3, 5	

(*Continues*)

Tool Description	References	QR Code
Wakelet https://wakelet.com/ A content curation platform where teachers and students can share information, including links, social media posts, videos, images, and text to organize information.	chapters 3, 5	
Wheel of Names https://wheelofnames.com/ The Wheel of Names is a name generator where you can input learners' names and then spin the wheel to identify a learner to participate. This would be used in a synchronous setting.	chapter 2	
When2Meet https://www.when2meet.com/ This free tool provides a way for teams to set up meetings and find common times to collaborate.	chapter 5	
Whiteboard.fi https://whiteboard.fi/ Free online whiteboard for teachers and students—provides a quick way to formatively assess student learning while engaging learners.	chapters 4, 6	
Wix https://www.wix.com Create, design, and manage your web presence. Learners can use a tool like Wix to create digital portfolios to showcase their work.	chapter 6	

Tool Description	References	QR Code
YouTube https://www.youtube.com/ YouTube can be used not only by teachers to share course content through video, but also by learners to share their learning.	chapters 1, 2	
Zoom https://zoom.us/ Video conferencing tool used to provide live sessions and record meetings; breakout rooms help support group collaboration.	chapters 1, 2, 4, 6	

REFERENCES

Aderibigbe, S. A. (2020). Online discussions as an intervention for strengthening students' engagement in general education. *Journal of Open Innovation*, *68*(4), 1–15. https://doi-org.neumann.idm.oclc.org/10.3390/joitmc6040098

Angelo, T. A., & Cross, K. P. (1993). *Classroom assessment techniques: A handbook for college teachers* (2nd ed.). Jossey-Bass.

Berge, Z. L. (2008). Changing instructor's roles in virtual worlds. *Quarterly Review of Distance Education*, *9*(4), 407–414. https://eric.ed.gov/?id=EJ875111

Bolliger, D. U., & Martin, F. (2018). Instructor and student perceptions of online student engagement strategies. *Distance Education*, *39*(4), 568–583. https://doi.org/10.1080/01587919.2018.1520041

Boston Consulting Group. (2018). *Making digital learning work*. https://edplus.asu.edu/sites/default/files/BCG-Making-Digital-Learning-Work-Apr-2018%20.pdf

Burbank, M., Kauchak, D. & A. J. Bates. (2010). Book clubs as professional development opportunities for preservice teacher candidates and practicing teachers: An exploratory study. *The New Educator*, *6*(1), 56–73. https://doi.org/10.1080/1547688X.2010.10399588

Center for Applied Special Technology. (2018). *Universal design for learning guidelines* (Version 2.2). http://udlguidelines.cast.org

Coyle, D. (2018). *The culture code: The secrets of highly successful groups*. Bantam.

Cunningham, J. (2010). Self-direction: A critical tool in distance learning. *Common Ground Journal*, *7*(2), 89–100. https://www.edcot.com/cmngrnd/backissues.html#v07n02

DeWitt, P. (2020, April 26). 6 reasons students aren't showing up for virtual learning. *Education Week*. https://www.edweek.org/leadership/opinion-6-reasons-students-arent-showing-up-for-virtual-learning/2020/04

Fahey, S., Moura, K., & Saarinen, J. (2019). *The educator's guide to Flipgrid eBook*. https://static.flipgrid.com/docs/Flipgrid_eBook_2nd_edition.pdf

Fletcher, K. (2020, October 28). Creating magic in your online course. *Faculty Focus*. https://www.facultyfocus.com/articles/online-education/creating-magic-in-your-online-classroom/

Flood, J., & Lapp, P. (1994). Teacher book clubs: Establishing literature discussion groups for teachers (issues and trends). *The Reading Teacher*, *47*(7), 574–576. https://www.jstor.org/stable/20201319

Fournier, E. (2019). *How to end a course: Teaching tips*. https://ctl.wustl.edu/how-to-end-a-course-teaching-tips/

Garrison, D. (2007). Online community of inquiry review: Social, cognitive, and teaching presence issues. *Journal of Asynchronous Learning Networks, 11*(1), 61–72. http://dx.doi.org/10.24059/olj.v11i1.1737

Garrison, D. R., Anderson, T., & Archer, W. (2000). Critical inquiry in a text-based environment: Computer conferencing in higher education. *Internet and Higher Education, 2*(2–3), 87–105. https://doi.org/10.1016/S1096-7516(00)00016-6

Garrison, D. R., Anderson, T., & Archer, W. (2001). Critical thinking, cognitive presence and computer conferencing in distance education. *American Journal of Distance Education, 15*(1), 7–23. https://doi.org/10.1080/08923640109527071

Garrison, D. R., & Arbaugh, J. B. (2007). Researching the community of inquiry framework: Review, issues, and future directions. *The Internet and Higher Education, 10*(3), 157–172. https://doi.org/10.1016/j.iheduc.2007.04.001

Gasper-Hulvat, M. (2018). "More like a real human being": Humanizing historical artists through remote service-learning. *Journal of Experiential Education, 41*(4), 397–410. https://doi.org/10.1177/1053825918808321

George, M. (2002). Professional development for a literature-based middle school curriculum. *The Clearing House, 75*(6), 327–331. https://www.jstor.org/stable/30189773

Golden, J. E. (2016). Supporting online faculty through communities of practice: Finding the faculty voice. *Innovations in Education & Teaching International, 53*(1), 84–93. http://dx.doi.org/10.1080/14703297.2014.910129

Hattie, J., & Timperley, H. (2007). The power of feedback. *Review of Educational Research, 77,* 81–112. doi 10.3102/003465430298487

Henrikson, R. (2020). Using online lectures to promote engagement: Recognising the self-directed learner as critical for practical inquiry. *Journal of Open, Flexible, & Distance Learning, 24*(1), 17–32. https://www.jofdl.nz/index.php/JOFDL/article/view/417

International Council for Open and Distance Education. (2018). *Global quality in online, open, flexible, and technology enhanced education.* https://olc-wordpress-assets.s3.amazonaws.com/uploads/2019/07/ICDE-Global-Quality-in-Online-Open-Flexible-and-Technology-Enhanced-Final-REPORT-2018.pdf

Islamoglu, H., Ay, O., Ilic, U., Mercimek, B., Donmez, P., Kuzu, A., & Odabasi, F. (2015). Infographics: A new competency area for teacher candidates. *Cypriot Journal of Educational Sciences, 10*(1), 32–39. https://un-pub.eu/ojs/index.php/cjes/issue/view/439

Jaggars, S., Edgecombe, N., & Stacey, G. W. (2013). *What we know about online course outcomes.* Columbia University, Teachers College, Community College Research Center.

Johnson, K., Powell, A., & Baker, S. (2018). Learning communities. In K. E. Linder (Ed.), *High Impact Practices in Online Education* (pp. 41–55). Stylus.

Jones, I. M. (2011). Can you see me now? Defining teaching presence in the online classroom through building a learning community. *Journal of Legal Studies Education, 28*(1), 67–116. https://doi.org/10.1111/j.1744-1722.2010.01085.x

Kilpatrick, J. R., Ehrlich, S., & Bartlett, M. (2021). Learning from COVID-19: Universal design for learning implementation prior to and during a pandemic. *The Journal of Applied Instructional Design, 10*(1). https://dx.doi.org/10.51869/101jkmbse

Kohan, N., Arabshahi, K. S., Mojtahedzadeh, R., Abbaszadeh, A., Rakhshani, T., & Emami, A. (2017). Self-directed learning barriers in a virtual environment: A qualitative study. *Journal of Advances in Medical Education & Professionalism, 5*(3), 116–123. https://www.ncbi.nlm.nih.gov/pmc/articles/PMC5522903/

Kuh, G. D., & O'Donnell, K. (2013). *Ensuring quality & taking high-impact practices to scale.* Association of American Colleges & Universities.

Loftin, D. (2018). *5 ways 3D models can help in education.* https://blogs.oregonstate.edu/inspire/2018/08/15/5-ways-3d-models-can-help-in-education/

McLaughlin Taddei, L., & Smith Budhai, S. (2016). Using voice-recorded reflections to increase cognitive presence in hybrid courses. *Journal of Digital Learning in Teacher Education, 32*(1), 38–46. https://doi.org/10.1080/21532974.2015.1111781

Mehta, R., Henriksen, D., & Rosenberg, J. M. (2019). It's not about the tools: Ed-tech training needs to go beyond specific tools and instead enable teachers with an adaptable, creative mindset. *Educational Leadership, 76*(5), 64–69. https://www.ascd.org/el/articles/its-not-about-the-tools

Miller, A. (2020). *Summative assessment in distance learning.* Edutopia. https://www.edutopia.org/article/summative-assessment-distance-learning

Montelongo, R. (2019). Less than/more than: Issues associated with high-impact online teaching and learning. *Administrative Issues Journal: Education, Practice & Research, 9*(1), 68–79. https://doi.org/10.5929/9.1.5

Newton-Calvert, Z. & Smith Arthur, D. (2018). Capstone courses and projects. In K. Linder & C. Mattison Hayes (Eds.), *High-impact practices in online education: Research and best practices* (pp. 165–182). Stylus.

Nicol, D. J., & Macfarlane-Dick, D. (2006). Formative assessment and self-regulated learning: A model and seven principles of good feedback practice. *Studies in Higher Education, 31*(2), 199–218. https://doi.org/10.1080/03075070600572090

Olenick, M., Flowers, M., Maltseva, T., & Diez-Sampedro, A. (2019). Research in academia: Creating and maintaining high performance research teams. *Nursing Research & Practice,* 1–3. https://doi.org/10.1155/2019/8423460

Online Learning Consortium. (2016). *Online Learning Consortium scorecards.* https://onlinelearningconsortium.org/consult/olc-quality-course-teaching-instructional-practice/

Ouyang, F., & Chang, Y. (2019). The relationships between social participatory roles and cognitive engagement levels in online discussions. *British Journal of Educational Technology, 50*(3), 1396–1414. https://doi.org/10.1111/bjet.12647

Peak Performance Center. (2021). *Chunking in learning.* https://thepeakperformancecenter.com/educational-learning/thinking/chunking/chunking-in-learning/

Peralta Community College District. (2020). *Peralta online equity rubric* (Version 3.0) [Creative Commons license: BY-SA]. https://web.peralta.edu/de/peralta-online-equity-initiative/equity/

Quality Matters. (2020). *Specific review standards from the QM higher education rubric* (6th ed.). https://www.qualitymatters.org/sites/default/files/PDFs/StandardsfromtheQMHigherEducationRubric.pdf

Rapanta, C., Botturi, L., Goodyear, P., Guàrdia, L., & Koole, M. (2020). Online university teaching during and after the Covid-19 crisis: Refocusing teacher presence and learning activity. *Postdigital Science and Education*, 2, 923–945. https://doi.org/10.1007/s42438-020-00155-y

Rappolt-Schlichtmann, G. (2020). *Distance learning: 6 UDL best practices for online learning*. Understood.org. https://www.understood.org/en/school-learning/for-educators/universal-design-for-learning/video-distance-learning-udl-best-practices

Sun, A., & Chen, X. (2016). Online education and its effective practice: A research review. *Journal of Information Technology Education*, 15, 157–190. http://www.informingscience.org/Publications/3502

U.S. Department of Education. (2017). *Reimagining the role of technology in higher education. A supplement to the National Education Technology Plan.*

Whitaker, T., Zoul, J., & Casas, J. (2015). *What connected educators do differently*. Routledge.

Yenawine, P. (1991). Thoughts on visual literacy. In J. Flood, S. B. Heath, & D. Lapp (Eds.), *Handbook of research on teaching literacy through the communicative and visual arts*. MacMillan Library Reference.

ABOUT THE AUTHORS

Joanne Ricevuto is the assistant vice president for instructional success and is responsible for the faculty programming at her institution, which includes providing and presenting a multitude of professional workshops to the faculty on various current topics in higher education. She also serves as the managing editor of the website for the Office of Instructional Success. She has been in higher education for 20+ years and is a professor of early childhood education. Additionally, she is the author of many published articles on virtual learning as well as student engagement. @DrRicevuto

Laura McLaughlin is a professor of education and teaches undergraduate and graduate courses. Laura has over 20 years of experience working with adult learners providing training, professional development, and coaching in corporate and educational settings. She is coauthor of *Increasing Engagement in Online Learning. Quick Reference Guide* (Association of Supervision and Curriculum Development, 2021), *Nurturing Young Innovators: Cultivating Creativity in the Home, School* (International Society for Technology in Education, 2017), *and Community* and *Teaching the 4 Cs with Technology: How Do I Teach 21st-Century Skills with 21st-Century Tools* (ASCD, 2015). @drlauramclaugh1

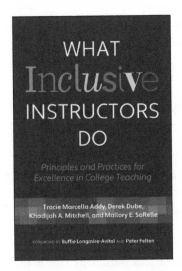

What Inclusive Instructors Do

Principles and Practices for Excellence in College Teaching

Tracie Marcella Addy, Derek Dube, Khadijah A. Mitchell, and Mallory E. SoRelle

Foreword by Buffie Longmire-Avital and Peter Felten

This book uniquely offers the distilled wisdom of scores of instructors across ranks, disciplines, and institution types, whose contributions are organized into a thematic framework that progressively introduces the reader to the key dispositions, principles, and practices for creating the inclusive classroom environments (in person and online) that will help their students succeed.

The authors asked the hundreds of instructors whom they surveyed as part of a national study to define what inclusive teaching meant to them and what inclusive teaching approaches they implemented in their courses.

The instructors' voices ring loudly as the authors draw on their responses, building on their experiences and expertise to frame the conversation about what inclusive teachers do. In addition, the authors describe their own insights and practices, integrating and discussing current literature relevant to inclusive teaching to ensure a research-supported approach.

Inclusive teaching is no longer an option but a vital teaching competency as our classrooms fill with racially diverse, first-generation, and low-income and working-class students who need a sense of belonging and recognition to thrive and contribute to the construction of knowledge.

The book unfolds as an informal journey that allows the reader to see into other teachers' practices. With questions for reflection embedded throughout the book, the authors provide the reader with an inviting and thoughtful guide to develop their own inclusive teaching practices.

99 Tips for Creating Simple and Sustainable Educational Videos

Karen Costa

Foreword by Michelle Pacansky-Brock

"Reading *99 Tips for Creating Simple and Sustainable Educational Videos* is like sitting down with an old friend and learning all of their best strategies for producing video content that will both help and motivate students in their learning. I loved the simplicity and practicality of Costa's suggestions and think that this is the perfect book for instructors who want to dip their toes in the video production waters, but are not sure where to start."—***Kathryn E. Linder***, *Executive Director of Program Development, Kansas State University Global Campus*

The research is clear: Online learning works best when faculty build regular, positive, and interactive relationships with students. A strategy that helps forge such a relationship is the use of videos. Student satisfaction and course engagement levels also increase with the use of instructor-generated videos—the subject of this book.

Beginning by outlining the different types of videos you can create, and what the research says about their effectiveness, Karen Costa explains how they can be designed to reinforce learning, to align with and promote course outcomes, and to save you time across your courses. She then describes how to create successful videos with commonly available technologies such as your smartphone without a major investment of time, demonstrating the simple steps she took to develop her bank of videos and build her confidence to deliver short, straightforward learning aids that are effective and personal.

Embedded QR codes in the text enable you to view sample videos and screencasts that bring the book's advice to life as you read.

If you've been wanting to include videos in your teaching but haven't found the time or confidence, this book will help you to develop a simple and sustainable video development process, supporting both your success and the success of your students.

Transforming Digital Learning and Assessment

Edited by Peggy L. Maki and Peter Shea

Foreword by Bryan Alexander

"This timely book proves essential for educational technologists, transformative for instructors, and critical for higher education's online learning leaders. Covering rich and relevant topics, the editors have crafted a book that captures the expansive opportunities, real challenges, and dynamic contexts for implementing emerging technologies with a solid mixture of theory, analysis, and examples."
—*Lance Eaton*, *Educational Programs Manager, Berkman Klein Center for Internet and Society, Harvard University*

Responding to both the trend toward increasing online enrollments as the demand for face-to-face education declines and to the immediate surge in remote learning owing to the COVID-19 pandemic, this book provides vital guidance to higher education institutions on how to develop faculty capacity to teach online and to leverage the affordances of an ever-increasing array of new and emerging learning technologies.

This book provides higher education leaders with the context they need to position their institutions in the changing online environment and with guidance to build support in a period of transition.

It is intended for campus leaders and administrators who work with campus teams charged with identifying learning technologies to meet agreed-upon program- or institution-level educational needs; for those coordinating across campus to build consensus on implementing online strategies; and for instructional designers, faculty developers, and assessment directors who assist departments and faculty effectively integrate learning technologies into their courses and programs. It will also appeal to faculty who take an active interest in improving online teaching.

Also available from Stylus

Designing the Online Learning Experience

Evidence-Based Principles and Strategies

Simone C. O. Conceição and Les L. Howles

Foreword by B. Jean Mandernach

"COVID-19 has pushed education at all levels over the tipping point for online education. This book provides an innovative framework and strategies that bring together user experience, human factors, and design thinking to create a model that wraps around the online learner. Conceição and Howles draw on their experiences as both scholars and practitioners to create a holistic way to think about learning. Both newcomers and experienced online instructors and designers will find creative solutions and strategies to make online teaching more engaging, personalized, and meaningful. In this book the authors share a map to the future of online teaching and learning."—*Michelle Glowacki-Dudka, Professor of Adult, Higher, and Community Education Educational Studies, Ball State University*

This book provides instructors with a holistic way of thinking about learners, learning, and online course design. The distinctive strategies derived from an integrated framework for designing the online learning experience help create an experience that is more personalized, engaging, and meaningful for online learners.

The focus of this book is on the learners and the design of their online learning experiences. The authors refer to learning design instead of instructional design—which focuses on instruction and places the instructor at the center stage of the process. Therefore, the focus is on approaching a learner's online course experience as a journey consisting of a combination of learning interactions with content, instructor, and other learners.

22883 Quicksilver Drive
Sterling, VA 20166-2019   Subscribe to our email alerts: www.Styluspub.com